STARTING POINTS

MEETING THE NEEDS OF OUR YOUNGEST CHILDREN

THE REPORT OF THE CARNEGIE TASK FORCE ON

MEETING THE NEEDS OF YOUNG CHILDREN

CARNEGIE CORPORATION OF NEW YORK

APRIL 1994

Carnegie Corporation of New York, 437 Madison Avenue, New York, NY 10022
Copyright © 1994 by Carnegie Corporation of New York. All rights reserved.
Printed in the United States of America

98 97 96 95 94   5 4 3 2

Library of Congress Cataloging-in-Publication Data

Carnegie Task Force on Meeting the Needs of Young Children.
      Starting points: meeting the needs of our youngest children:
      the report of the Carnegie Task Force on Meeting the Needs
      of Young Children.
p.   cm.
"April 1994"
Includes bibliographical references and index.
ISBN 1-885039-00-X
1. Child welfare–United States. 2. Toddlers–Services for–United States.
3. Infants–Services for–United States.
I. Carnegie Corporation of New York. II. Title.
HV741.C3364   1994
362.7′0973–dc20   94-8825
                                                         CIP

Copies of this report may be obtained from:

Carnegie Corporation of New York
P.O. Box 753
Waldorf, MD 20604

The price for single copies is $10.00, including shipping and handling.
All orders must be prepaid by check or money order.
Bulk rates available; for more information, please telephone (212) 371-3200.

CARNEGIE TASK FORCE ON MEETING THE NEEDS OF YOUNG CHILDREN

Staff of the Carnegie Task Force on Meeting the Needs of Young Children

Linda A. Randolph
Executive Director
   (through September 1993)

Kathryn Taaffe Young
Director of Studies

Jeannette L. Aspden
Editor for Special Projects

Jeanmarie Holtsford
Administrative Assistant
   (through July 1993)

Bonnie J. Piller
Secretary

Laura K. Hankin
Research Assistant
   (through January 1994)

Staff of Carnegie Corporation of New York

David A. Hamburg
President

Vivien Stewart
Program Chair

Elena O. Nightingale
Special Advisor to the President and
   Senior Program Officer

Michael H. Levine
Program Officer

Nidia Marti
Administrative Assistant

Sara K. Wolpert
Secretary

CONTENTS

FOREWORD   vii

PREFACE   ix

EXECUTIVE SUMMARY   xiii

PART I: THE QUIET CRISIS

The Quiet Crisis   3
Reversing a Pattern of Neglect   5
The Critical Importance of the First Three Years   6
Striking Changes in the American Family   12
A National Investment   18
A Family-Centered Approach   22

PART II: STARTING POINTS FOR OUR YOUNGEST CHILDREN

Promote Responsible Parenthood   25
Promote Planned Childbearing   26
Ensure Comprehensive Prenatal Care and Support   32
Provide Opportunities for Parent Education and Support   36

Guarantee Quality Child Care Choices   43
Improve Parental Leave Benefits   44
Ensure Quality Child Care for Infants and Toddlers   48
Provide Parents with Affordable Child Care Options   56
Develop Networks of Family-Centered Child Care Programs
    for Infants and Toddlers   60

Ensure Good Health and Protection   63
The Scope of Health Care for Very Young Children   64
Provide Needed Health Care Services for All Infants and Toddlers   68
Protect Young Children from Injury and Promote Their Health   73
Create Safe Environments for Young Children   76

Mobilize Communities to Support Young Children
and Their Families   85
    Communities Count 86
    Promote a Culture of Responsibility 88
    Move Toward Family-Centered Communities 93
    Reinvent Government 99
    Getting Down to Work 102

PART III: A NEW VISION: RECOMMENDATIONS FOR ACTION

A New Vision: Recommendations for Action   105
    Promote Responsible Parenthood 106
    Guarantee Quality Child Care Choices 106
    Ensure Good Health and Protection 108
    Mobilize Communities to Support Young Children
       and Their Families 109
    A Call to Action 110

APPENDIXES

    A. Consultants to the Task Force 114
    B. Papers Commissioned by the Task Force 115
    C. Invitees, "Services That Work" Meeting,
       January 27–28, 1993 116
    D. Biographies of Task Force Members and Staff 118

REFERENCES   124

INDEX OF PROGRAMS   131

FOREWORD

In the United States today—probably the most technologically advanced, affluent, and democratic society the world has ever known—the crucially formative years of early childhood have become a time of peril and loss for millions of children and their families. Now, however, there is an opportunity to prevent much of this damage. A remarkable degree of consensus is emerging on the essential requirements that positively influence a child's early growth and development as well as on the ways that parents and others can provide our youngest children with a healthy start.

The human being experiences a prolonged period of immaturity and vulnerability—the longest of any known species. During the first three years of life, much has to be acquired, much mastered, much tried and found wanting, much discovered and put to use. Ideally, this learning time is spent in close relationship with adults who offer nurturing love, protection, guidance, stimulation, and support. For the caregivers, it is an enduring, long-term, highly challenging commitment. Rearing by a few caring, responsive, dependable adults leads to strong attachments and provides a secure base from which the infant can explore the larger social and physical world. Such secure early attachments are essential for human development.

Historically, several requirements have been valuable for healthy child development:

- An intact, cohesive, nuclear family, dependable under stress
- A relationship with at least one parent who is consistently nurturing, loving, enjoying, teaching, and coping
- Easy access to supportive extended family members
- A supportive community, whether it be a neighborhood, religious, ethnic, or political group
- Parents exposed to childrearing during the years of their own growth and development through explicit and implicit education for parenthood
- A perception of opportunity during childhood with a tangible basis for hope of an attractive future
- Predictability about the adult environment that enables a child to take advantage of opportunities in the environment

The ancient and fundamental desire of parents to do well by their children has not changed, but the setting is now quite different. Economic, social, and demographic pressures affect American families powerfully. In the past three decades—a moment in human history—the change in regular patterns of contact between American children and their adult relatives is remarkable. Not only are their mothers home much less, but there is little if any evidence that fathers spend more time with their children, and grandparents, too, are largely absent from the daily life of most children. Nor is quality child care sufficiently available to fill the gap. Powerful institutions of society such as business and government have done little to strengthen families in the rapidly changing circumstances of the late 20th century.

If some traditional sources of stability and support have become weakened by enormous historical changes, then how can young children's development best be nurtured? The pivotal institutions are the family, the health care system, the emerging child care system, religious institutions, community organizations, and the media.

Building on its long-standing concern with the healthy development of children and youth, Carnegie Corporation of New York in 1991 established the Carnegie Task Force on Meeting the Needs of Young Children. The mission of the task force was to develop a report that would provide a framework of scientific knowledge and offer an action agenda to ensure the healthy development of children from before birth to age three. The thirty members of the task force are leaders of various sectors of American life—business, science, media, education, economics, health, child development, and the law. They looked intensively at the major influences affecting the development of children in the first three years of life. This distinguished group has proceeded with great vigor, understanding, and foresight. The report is broadly integrative, bringing together information from many different sources and recommending actions that cut across existing barriers. The focus is consistently on the experience of growing up as well as the experience of parents and others who care for our youngest children. The report shows clearly how the first few years can be put to good use for child development, health, education, and positive human relationships.

I want to express my heartfelt gratitude to the task force for their vital contribution to the well-being of the nation's youngest children. In particular, I must single out a few people who made special contributions in leadership roles: the first chairman, Richard W. Riley, now secretary of education; the co-chairmen, Eleanor E. Maccoby and Julius B. Richmond; and Carnegie staff members Michael H. Levine, Elena O. Nightingale, Linda A. Randolph, Vivien Stewart, and above all Kathryn Taaffe Young. In years to come, people everywhere who care about children will have reason to share my appreciation.

If the American people come to understand what this report says and why, prospects for the nation's future will improve. If there is anything more fundamental than a decent start in life, I wonder what it could be.

DAVID A. HAMBURG
President, Carnegie Corporation of
    New York

This report draws attention to a much-neglected period of childhood: the first three years of life. Although research in the past thirty years has greatly enriched our knowledge of the importance of this period, arrangements for the care and nurturance of our youngest children have not kept pace. Indeed, the life situation of many of these youngest children has deteriorated badly. This report outlines what we know about the requirements for optimal development during this period, considers the ways in which society might reverse the deteriorating trends, and describes the necessary conditions for families to function well in the interests of their young children.

Human infants usually come into the world with a well-organized capacity for adapting to their environment. Much of this capacity is attributable to our unique central nervous system. But the unfolding of the developing brain is not inevitable. It depends on a fostering environment, one that is reasonably stable while at the same time stimulating, responsive, protective, and loving.

When nurturing conditions are absent, the baby becomes apathetic and loses weight. Pediatricians refer to this as "failure to thrive." This condition is easy to recognize, but less extreme forms of environmental deficiency can have negative effects that may go unnoticed but that may nevertheless threaten the child's

future. In the second and third years of life, the teaching begins that enables children to respect the rights of others and restrain impulsive behavior that is potentially disruptive to others. Daily, even hourly, prosocial "lessons" need to be interwoven with nurturance if the child is to become sufficiently social to take advantage of later learning opportunities.

Because the family is the main provider of the environment of the infant and toddler, it is clear that the family's care of the young child largely determines the child's early progress. Our attention to supporting the development of the child, therefore, must focus on family members: on their commitment to the child, their availability, and their resources. But families do not function in a vacuum. The context in which they rear children—their economic, social, and community supports—has much to do with their effectiveness.

Preserving the fabric of any society requires the continuous replacement of older generations by adequately prepared younger ones. The society as a whole, and individual families within it, must provide the conditions that allow children to progress toward competent adulthood. The earliest years of life thus lay the foundation for all that follows. Research has given us rich knowledge of development during this period, but we are applying this knowledge very poorly. Infant mortality rates are too high, child immunization rates are too low. As the nation's governors remind us, too many children arrive at school—or even at preschool—ill prepared to learn. More children are born into poverty (now almost 25 percent of children); more children are in substandard care while their parents work; and more children are being reared by single parents. All these conditions increase the risks that children will not be adequately prepared, by the end of their first three years, for the next phase of development.

Awareness has been growing that this "quiet crisis" in the lives of so many young children threatens not only the children themselves, but also our future as a nation. In 1991, recognizing the urgency of the situation, David A. Hamburg, the president of Carnegie Corporation of New York, appointed the Task Force on Meeting the Needs of Young Children, charging it to focus on the earliest period of children's lives: from the prenatal period to age three. This judgment reflected the fact that this age period is perhaps the most neglected. There are no clearly defined institutions such as preschools or schools to serve it. Instead, agencies that serve young children and their families are disparate, with health, welfare, educational, and social service agencies working independently and sometimes at cross-purposes. The establishment of the task force also reflected the importance of this earliest age

period as a time for establishing the foundation of future healthy development. The task force recognizes, of course, that a good start during these earliest years will not immunize a child against all the problems that may befall it at later times; a good start does, however, improve the chances that the child will be equipped to surmount future difficulties.

While we recognize that all families need some educational and social supports, clearly some families are in greater need than others. Of necessity, therefore, the report focuses on the more needy families. We believe, however, that the nation needs to be vigilant about the well-being of *all* its young children.

Neither the problems facing families nor the solutions to those problems can be neatly compartmentalized. In families under stress, problems do not come singly, and they are linked in complex ways. These complexities brought the task force to conclude that any proposed solutions must rest on comprehensive approaches. No single service system can deal with the multiple problems many families face. And clearly, no one model will meet the needs of all. There cannot be a single federal, state, local, or private sector solution. Rather, resources and commitment from all these levels and sectors will be necessary.

Through this report, we hope to raise the level of consciousness of the nation concerning the plight of families rearing young children.

Among the many challenges that face our nation, we feel that none should have higher priority than the adversity that many such families face. Some of the major risk factors that endanger young children and their families—poverty, poor-quality child care, violence in the streets—are not amenable to easy or immediate solutions. Still, there are things that can be done in the immediate future to begin to reverse the alarming trends. This report focuses on what is possible, given current resources and the will to mobilize them. We can do no less than set to work on this agenda. Our nation's future is at stake.

. . . .

As the co-chairmen of the task force, we wish to acknowledge the devotion of its members to the work of the group. They contributed their time and expertise in more ways than we can adequately describe. We should note that, because of the complexity of issues considered, concluding our work was no easy task. The pervasive mutual respect among members enabled us to come to a consensus. We are grateful to each of them.

Several individual acknowledgments are in order. We are indebted to Secretary of Education Richard Riley, who served as the task force's first chair. His leadership helped in establishing the task force and in charting our early work. We are fortunate that he has gone on to serve us all as the secretary of education. We are also indebted to Isabel Sawhill and Michael Wald, who left us to take up appointments in the Clinton Administration, and to Ramon Cortines, who left to become Chancellor of the Board of Education of the City of New York.

To Kathryn Taaffe Young, who served as director of studies and who was the primary author of the report, we are all profoundly grateful. Out of our often rambling and diffuse discussions, she found coherence and lucidity and has created an art form to admire.

We also add a note of appreciation to Linda Randolph, who served as the executive director of the task force until her return to Mount Sinai School of Medicine in September 1993. We are grateful for the guidance and support of the Carnegie Corporation steering committee, which included David Hamburg, Elena Nightingale, Michael Levine, and Vivien Stewart. We are particularly grateful to Michael Levine for his major contribution to the report.

Other Carnegie Corporation staff members deserve special recognition. Jeannette Aspden edited the report and managed the publication process. Laura Hankin provided research assistance throughout the life of the task force. The task force particularly wishes to acknowledge the invaluable contribution of Bonnie Piller, who typed all the many drafts of the report and whose tireless efforts and cheerful manner made the task force's work run smoothly. In addition, Nidia Marti, Sara Wolpert, Kathleen Sheridan, and Georganne Brown provided behind-the-scenes support.

The task force is grateful to the authors of commissioned papers and to the participants in the January 1993 meeting on "Services That Work" (see Appendixes B and C). Larry Aber, Sarah Brown, Joan Lombardi, Ellen Galinsky, Terry Bond, Eleanor Szanton, Carol Berman, Helen Blank, Emily Fenichel, and Ruby Takanishi reviewed drafts of the report and offered advice on ways to improve its structure and substance.

Joseph Foote, Robert Hodapp, and Rima Shore each provided valuable editorial assistance in all parts of the report, and Sally Janin and Cynthia Cliff of Janin Design Communication brought insight and inspiration to the design of the report.

And lastly we acknowledge the leadership of the Corporation's president, David A. Hamburg, in conceiving the idea of a task force. He showed his characteristic vision, imagination, and courage in marshaling Carnegie's resources to tackle one of the most important and complex problems facing this nation.

ELEANOR E. MACCOBY
Department of Psychology
Stanford University
Stanford, California

JULIUS B. RICHMOND
Department of Social Medicine
Harvard Medical School
Boston, Massachusetts

Our nation's infants and toddlers and their families are in trouble. Compared with most other industrialized countries, the United States has a higher infant mortality rate, a higher proportion of low-birthweight babies, a smaller proportion of babies immunized against childhood diseases, and a much higher rate of babies born to adolescent mothers. Of the twelve million children under the age of three in the United States today, a staggering number are affected by one or more risk factors that undermine healthy development. One in four lives in poverty. One in four lives in a single-parent family. One in three victims of physical abuse is a baby under the age of one.

These numbers reflect a pattern of neglect that must be reversed. It has long been known that the first years of life are crucial for later development, and recent scientific findings provide a basis for these observations. We can now say, with greater confidence than ever before, that the quality of young children's environment and social experience has a decisive, long-lasting impact on their well-being and ability to learn.

The risks are clearer than ever before: an adverse environment can compromise a young child's brain function and overall development, placing him or her at greater risk of developing a variety of cognitive, behavioral, and physical difficulties. In some cases these effects may be irreversible. But the opportunities are equally dramatic: adequate pre- and postnatal care, dependable caregivers, and strong community support can prevent damage and provide a child with a decent start in life.

Researchers have thoroughly documented the importance of the pre- and postnatal months and the first three years, but a wide gap remains between scientific knowledge and social policy. Today, changes in the American economy and family, combined with the lack of affordable health and child care and the crumbling of other family supports, make it increasingly difficult for parents to provide the essential requirements for their young children's healthy development.

More than half of mothers of children under the age of three work outside the home. This is a matter of concern because minimal parental leave is available at the time of birth, and child care for infants and toddlers is often hard to find and of poor quality. Most parents feel overwhelmed by the dual demands of work and family, have less time to spend with their children, and worry about the unreliable and substandard child care in which many infants and toddlers spend long hours. These problems affect all families, but for families living in poverty, the lack of prenatal and child health care, human services, and social support in increasingly violent neighborhoods further stacks the deck against their children.

These facts add up to a crisis that jeopardizes our children's healthy development, undermines school readiness, and ultimately threatens our nation's economic strength. Once a world leader and innovator in education, the United States today is making insufficient investments in its future workforce—our youngest children. In contrast to all the other leading industrialized nations, the United States fails to give parents time to be with their newborns, fails to ensure pre- and postnatal health care for mothers and infants, and fails to provide adequate child care.

The crisis among our youngest children and their families is a quiet crisis. After all, babies seldom make the news. Their parents—often young people struggling to balance their home and work responsibilities—tend to have little economic clout and little say in community affairs. Moreover, children's early experience is associated with the home—a private realm into which many policymakers have been reluctant to intrude.

The problems facing our youngest children and their families cannot be solved through piecemeal efforts; nor can they be solved entirely through governmental programs and business initiatives. All Americans must take responsibility for reversing the quiet crisis. As the risks to our children intensify, so must our determination to enact family-centered programs and policies to ensure all of our youngest children the decent start that they deserve.

RECOMMENDATIONS FOR ACTION

The task force concluded that reversing the quiet crisis calls for action in four key areas that constitute vital starting points for our youngest children and their families.

Promote Responsible Parenthood

Our nation must foster both personal and social responsibility for having children. To enable women and men to plan and act responsibly, we need a national commitment to making comprehensive family planning, pre-conception, prenatal, and postpartum health services available, and to providing much more community-based education about the responsibilities of parenthood. To promote responsible parenthood, the task force recommends

- Planning for parenthood by all couples to avoid unnecessary risks and to promote a healthy environment for raising a child
- Providing comprehensive family planning, pre-conception, prenatal, and postpartum services as part of a minimum health care reform package.
- Delaying adolescent pregnancy through the provision of services, counseling, support, and age-appropriate life options
- Expanding education about parenthood in families, schools, and communities, beginning in the elementary school years but no later than early adolescence
- Directing state and local funds to initiate and expand community-based parent education and support programs for families with infants and toddlers

Guarantee Quality Child Care Choices

For healthy development, infants and toddlers need a continuing relationship with a few caring people, beginning with their parents and later including other child care providers. If this contact is substantial and consistent, young children can form the trusting attachments that are needed for healthy development throughout life. Infants and toddlers should develop these relationships in safe and predictable environments—in their homes or in child care settings. To guarantee quality child care choices the task force recommends

- Strengthening the Family and Medical Leave Act of 1993 by expanding coverage to include employers with fewer than fifty employees, extending the twelve-week leave to four to six months, and providing partial wage replacement
- Adopting family-friendly workplace policies such as flexible work schedules and assistance with child care
- Channeling substantial new federal funds into child care to ensure quality and affordability for families with children under three and making the Dependent Care Tax Credit refundable for low- and moderate-income families
- Providing greater incentives to states to adopt and monitor child care standards of quality
- Developing community-based networks linking all child care programs and offering parents a variety of child care settings

- Allocating federal and state funds to provide training opportunities so that all child care providers have a grounding in the care and development of children under three
- Improving salary and benefits for child care providers

Ensure Good Health and Protection

When young children are healthy, they are more likely to succeed in school and, in time, to form a more productive workforce and become better parents. Few social programs offer greater long-term benefits for American society than guaranteeing good health care for all infants and toddlers. Good health involves more than health care services. Being healthy means that young children are able to grow up in safe homes and neighborhoods. To ensure good health and protection, the task force recommends

- Making comprehensive primary and preventive care services, including immunizations, available to infants and toddlers as part of a minimum benefits package in health care reform
- Offering home-visiting services to all first-time mothers with a newborn and providing comprehensive home visiting services by trained professionals to all families who are at risk for poor maternal and child health outcomes
- Expanding the Women, Infants and Children (WIC) nutritional supplementation program to serve all eligible women and children
- Making the reduction of unintentional injuries to infants and toddlers a national priority

- Expanding proven parent education, support, and counseling programs to teach parents nonviolent conflict resolution in order to prevent child abuse and neglect, and implementing community-based programs to help families and children cope with the effects of living in unsafe and violent communities
- Enacting national, state, and local laws that stringently control the possession of firearms

Mobilize Communities to Support Young Children and Their Families

Broad-based community supports and services are necessary to ensure a decent start for our youngest children. Unfortunately, community services for families with children under three are few and fragmentary. To reverse the crisis facing families with young children, the old ways of providing services and supports must be reassessed, and broad, integrated approaches must be found to ensure that every family with a newborn is linked to a source of health care, child care, and parenting support. To mobilize communities to support young children and their families, the task force recommends

- Focusing the attention of every community in America on the needs of children under three and their families, by initiating a community-based strategic planning process
- Experimenting broadly with the creation of family-centered communities through two promising approaches: creating family and child centers to provide services and supports for all families; and expanding and adapting the Head Start model to meet the needs of low-income families with infants and toddlers
- Creating a high-level federal group, directed by the President to coordinate federal agency support on behalf of young children and to remove the obstacles faced by states and communities in their attempts to provide more effective services and supports to families with young children
- Funding family-centered programs through the Community Enterprise Board in order to strengthen families with infants and toddlers
- Establishing mechanisms, at the state level, to adopt comprehensive policy and program plans that focus on the period before birth through the first three years of a child's life

A Call to Action

The task force calls upon all sectors of American society to join together to ensure the healthy development of our nation's youngest children.

- We ask the *President* to direct a high-level federal group to review the findings of this report and to ensure the adequacy, coherence, and coordination of federal policies and programs for families with young children.
- We urge *federal agencies* to identify and remove the obstacles that states and communities encounter as they implement federally funded programs or test innovative solutions.

- We call upon *states* to review their legislative and regulatory frameworks, particularly with regard to child care, in order to raise the quality of services for children under the age of three.

- We call upon *community leaders* to assess the adequacy of existing services for families with young children (especially those with multiple risks), to recommend steps to improve and coordinate services, and to introduce mechanisms for monitoring results.

- We call upon the *private and philanthropic sectors*, including foundations, to pay more attention to families with children under three and to expand their support of initiatives that give our youngest children a decent start in life.

- We urge *educators*, to incorporate services to children under age three in their plans for the schools of the twenty-first century, to increase their efforts to educate young people about parenthood, and to provide more training and technical assistance to child care providers.

- We call upon *health care decision makers* to include, in any plan for national health care reform, comprehensive prenatal care for expectant mothers and universal primary and preventive care for young children and to consider establishing a specific standard of coverage and service for young children.

- We urge *service providers* in child care, health, and social services to work together by taking a family-centered approach to meeting the needs of young children and the adults who care for them. We ask them to offer staff, parents, and other caregivers opportunities to learn more about the needs of families with young children, about child development, and about promoting children's health and safety.

- We call upon *business leaders* to support policies that result in family-friendly workplaces in businesses of every size, for example strengthening the Family and Medical Leave Act of 1993 and introducing flexible work schedules.

- We call upon the *media* to deliver strong messages about responsible motherhood and fatherhood, to promote recognition of the importance of the first three years, and to give us all insight into the quiet crisis.

- We call upon *mothers and fathers* to secure the knowledge and resources they need to plan and raise children responsibly. When these resources are not available, we urge them to make their needs known to government representatives, community leaders, and service providers.

All Americans must work together, in their homes, workplaces, and communities, to ensure that children under the age of three—our most vulnerable citizens—are given the care and protection they need and deserve. Nothing less than the well-being of our society and the future of its vital institutions is at stake.

THE HOPE THAT IS BORN ANEW IN
EACH NEW CHILD MUST BE CULTIVATED
AND NURTURED.
— JONAS SALK

A cross the United States, we are beginning to hear the rumblings of a quiet crisis. Our nation's children under the age of three and their families are in trouble, and their plight worsens every day. To be sure, the children themselves are not quiet; they are crying out for help. And their parents' anxieties about inadequate child care and the high cost of their child's health care can be heard in kitchens, playgrounds, pediatricians' waiting rooms, and workplace cafeterias across the nation. But these sounds rarely become sound-bites. Babies seldom make the news: they do not commit crimes, do drugs, or drop out of school. We don't hear interviews with parents as they anguish over finding decent, affordable child care; we don't notice the unmet prenatal needs of expectant mothers. Policymakers are rarely forced to contend with these realities. And so, the problems of our youngest children and their parents remain a quiet crisis.

Consider the state of America's youngest children and their families. In 1993 the National Educational Goals Panel reported that nearly half of our infants and toddlers start life at a disadvantage and do not have the supports necessary to grow and thrive.[1] A significant number of children under three confront one or more major risk factors:

- *Inadequate prenatal care.* Nearly a quarter of all of pregnant women in America, many of whom are adolescents, receive little or no prenatal care. Many of these pregnancies are unintended: the United States has the highest rate of unintended pregnancy in the industrialized world.

- *Isolated parents.* More divorces, more single-parent families, and less familial and community support have made parents feel more isolated than ever before in raising their young children.

- *Substandard child care.* More than half (53 percent) of mothers return to the workforce within a year of the baby's birth. High-quality child care settings are scarce, and many infants and toddlers spend thirty-five or more hours per week in substandard child care.

THE QUIET CRISIS

Of the 12 million children under the age of three in the United States today, a staggering number are affected by one or more risk factors that make healthy development more difficult.

CHANGES IN FAMILY STRUCTURE ARE TROUBLING

- In 1960, only 5 percent of all births in the United States were to unmarried mothers; by 1988, the proportion had risen to 26 percent.
- About every minute, an American adolescent has a baby; every year, about 1 million adolescents become pregnant.
- Divorce rates are rising: In 1960, less than one percent of children experienced their parents' divorce each year; by 1986, the percentage had more than doubled, and by 1993 almost half of all children could expect to experience a divorce during childhood and to live an average of five years in a single-parent family.
- Children are increasingly likely to live with just one parent, usually the mother: In 1960, fewer than 10 percent of all children under the age of eighteen lived with one parent; by 1989 almost a quarter of all children lived with one parent. Fathers are increasingly absent from the home.

MANY YOUNG CHILDREN LIVE IN POVERTY

- One in four infants and toddlers under the age of three (nearly 3 million children) live in families with incomes below the federal poverty level.
- While the number of children under six increased by less than 10 percent between 1971 and 1991, the number of poor children under six increased by more than 60 percent.

MORE CHILDREN LIVE IN FOSTER HOMES

- From 1987 to 1991, the number of children in foster care jumped by more than 50 percent—from 300,000 in 1987 to 460,000 in 1991.
- Babies under the age of one are the fastest growing category of children entering foster care, according to a study conducted in New York and Illinois.

INFANTS AND TODDLERS ARE SPENDING LESS TIME WITH THEIR PARENTS

- Pressures on both parents to work mean that they have less time with their young children; more than half of mothers of infants now work outside the home.
- More than 5 million children under the age of three are in the care of other adults while their parents work. Much child care for infants and toddlers is of substandard quality, whether it is provided by centers, family child care homes, or relatives.

HEALTH DATA ARE DISCOURAGING

- In the United States, nine out of every thousand infants die before age one—a mortality rate higher than that of 19 other nations.
- The mortality rate is higher for infants born in minority families: African American babies are twice as likely to die within the first year of life as white babies.
- In 1992, rates of immunization against common childhood diseases among two-year-olds were only 30 percent in some states; in most states, they were below 60 percent.

PHYSICAL ABUSE, NEGLECT, AND UNINTENTIONAL INJURY ARE COMMON

- One in three victims of physical abuse is a baby—less than a year old. In 1990, more one-year-olds were maltreated than in any previous year for which we have data.
- Almost 90 percent of children who died of abuse and neglect in 1990 were under the age of five; 53 percent were less than a year old.
- The leading cause of death among children aged one to four is unintentional injury.

SOURCES:
America's children: Economic perspectives and policy options. *Science* 255:41–46, 1992.
Children's Defense Fund. *The State of America's Children 1992.* Washington, DC, 1992.
D. Daro and K. McCurdy. Current Trends in Abuse Reporting and Fatalities: The Results of the 1990 Annual Fifty-State

Survey. Chicago: National Committee for the Prevention of Child Abuse, 1990.

S. D. Einbinder. A Statistical Profile of Children Living in Poverty: Children under Three and Children under Six, 1990. Unpublished document from the National Center for Children in Poverty. New York: Columbia University School of Public Health, 1992.

N. Goldstein. Are Changes in Work and Family Harming Children? Background paper prepared for the Task Force on Meeting the Needs of Young Children, Carnegie Corporation of New York, January 1993.

Alan Guttmacher Institute. Facts in Brief: Teenage Sexual and Reproductive Behavior. New York, July 15, 1993.

E. M. Hetherington and W. G. Clingempeel. Coping with marital transitions: A family systems perspective. *Monographs of the Society for Research in Child Development* 57:2–3, 1992.

R. Marshall. *The State of Families, 3: Losing Direction, Families, Human Resource Development, and Economic Performance.* Milwaukee, WI: Family Service America, 1991.

National Center for Health Statistics. Advance report of Final Mortality Statistics 1991. *Vital Statistics of the United States, Volume 1.* Washington, DC: U.S. Department Health and Human Services, 1991.

National Center for Health Statistics. *Prevention Profile. Health, United States, 1991.* Hyattsville, MD: Public Health Service, 1992.

National Center for Children in Poverty. Five Million Children: 1992 Update. New York: Columbia School of Public Health, 1992.

I. V. Sawhill. Young children and families. In *Setting Domestic Priorities: What Can Government Do?* Washington, DC: The Brookings Institution, 1992.

T. Tahara. Research Notes: U.S. Child Substitute Care Flow Data for Fiscal Year 1992 and Current Trends in the State Child Substitute Care Populations. Washington, DC: American Public Welfare Association, 1993.

U.S. Bureau of the Census. Marital status and living arrangements: March 1988. *Current Population Reports,* Series P-20, Number 433, 1989.

U.S. Bureau of the Census. *Statistical Abstracts of the United States, 1991,* Table 70. Washington, DC, 1991.

U.S. Department of Health and Human Services. National Child Abuse and Neglect Data System. Working paper 1. Publication Number (ACF) 92-30361. Washington, DC, 1992.

B. Willer, S. L. Hofferth, E. E. Kisker, P. Divine-Hawkins, E. Farquar, and F. B. Glantz. *The Demand and Supply of Child Care in 1990: Joint Findings from The National Child Care Survey 1990 and a Profile of Child Care Settings.* Washington, DC: National Association for the Education of Young Children, 1991.

L. B. Williams and W. F. Pratt. Wanted and unwanted childbearing in the United States: 1973–88. Data from the National Survey of Family Growth. *Advance Data from Vital and Health Statistics* no. 189. Hyattsville, MD: National Center for Health Statistics, 1990.

F. Wulczyn and R. George. Foster care in New York and Illinois: The challenge of rapid change. *Social Service Review* 66:278–294, 1992.

- *Poverty.* Almost a quarter (24.9 percent) of families with children under age three live in poverty. The large majority of these families are headed by one parent, usually the mother. These families often live in unsafe neighborhoods, and have poor access to quality child care, health services, or family support programs.

- *Insufficient stimulation.* Only half (50 percent) of infants and toddlers are routinely read to by their parents, and many parents do not engage in other activities to stimulate their young child's intellectual development. It is not surprising, then, that teachers report that 35 percent of American kindergarten children arrive at school unprepared to learn.

These numbers add up to a crisis that, though quiet, threatens to undermine our nation's economic strength and competitiveness. The Carnegie Task Force on Meeting the Needs of Young Children urges a national response. We call upon all Americans and America's vital institutions to focus attention on our youngest children and their families, and to adopt new initiatives to respond to their problems. They have an urgent need for our compassion and our help, and we, as a nation, have an incalculable stake in their well-being.

REVERSING A PATTERN OF NEGLECT

This report has two related aims. First, we document the conditions of children and their families from the prenatal period to age three. We seek to focus attention on the importance of the first three years of life, and to describe how the nation neglects children in this age group. Second, we offer realistic, workable measures for ameliorating the problems we document. Many of these measures are already in place on the local level and have proved successful there. They need only be adapted and expanded to help young children and their families throughout the country.

The problems we describe are many, and they are massive; not one lends itself to a simple solution. But the task force has proceeded from the assumption that, given sufficient focus and sufficient political will, America can begin to find its way toward solutions. We can formulate and implement social policy that responds, over time, to the most urgent needs of our young children and their families. We can begin to reverse a pattern of neglect.

But that effort requires discipline. When the task force undertook this journey, it knew that it could not explore every road or follow every byway; it could not afford to be all over the map. Instead, it selected, based on extensive research and deliberation, four starting points that seemed likely to move our nation toward the goal of giving all children the early experience they need to reach their full potential and ensuring that no child falls between the cracks.

Persuaded that strong families and communities are essential to successful development in this early period, the task force chose these starting points: promoting responsible parenthood; guaranteeing quality child care choices; ensuring good health and protection; and mobilizing communities to support young children and their families.

This report provides no single answer, no single solution to the many problems facing children under three and their families. Nor does it focus its recommended actions on a single segment of our society: all of us must work together. If we do, we as a nation can be more

than compassionate. We can also realize our common values: strong families and communities, an informed citizenry, a productive workforce, and a competitive and sound economy. Investing in these first three years is fundamentally necessary for children themselves, for their families, and for our nation. It is time to sound—and answer—the alarm about the neglect of our nation's young children and their families.

THE CRITICAL IMPORTANCE OF THE FIRST THREE YEARS

How individuals function from the preschool years all the way through adolescence and even adulthood hinges, to a significant extent, on their experiences before the age of three. Researchers have thoroughly documented the importance of the pre- and postnatal months and the first three years, but a wide gap remains between scientific knowledge and social policy. This is particularly true in two areas: our policies reflect neither our growing knowledge of early brain development nor our understanding of factors that tend to protect young children or place them at risk.

The Developing Brain

Parents and experts have long known that babies raised by caring adults in safe and stimulating environments are better learners than those raised in less stimulating settings and that the effects can be long-lasting. Recent scientific findings provide a basis for these observations: Over the past decade, scientists have gained new insights into molecular biology that illuminate the workings of the nervous system. At the same time, they have acquired powerful research tools, including sophisticated brain scans that allow them to study the developing brain in greater detail, and with greater precision, than ever before. Brain scans also allow scientists to measure the impact of the environment on brain function.

This research points to five key findings that should inform policymakers' deliberations on early childhood policy:

- *First, the brain development that takes place before age one is more rapid and extensive than we previously realized.*

Positron emission tomography (PET) studies show that the biochemical patterns of a one-year-old's brain qualitatively resemble those of the normal young adult.[2] This is astonishing, considering the immense scale of early brain development. From a few initial cells, the brain develops billions of brain cells, or neurons, over a period of several months. And once these neurons are formed, they must migrate to their correct locations.[3]

Brain cell formation is virtually complete before birth, but brain maturation is far from over: the next challenge is the formation of connections among these cells—up to 15,000 connections, or synapses, per neuron. These synapses form the brain's physical "maps" that allow learning to take place. We now know that in the months after birth, this process proceeds with astounding rapidity, as the number of synapses increases twentyfold, from 50 trillion to 1,000 trillion.[4]

- *Second, brain development is much more vulnerable to environmental influence than we ever suspected.*

We have long understood that factors other than genetic programming affect brain development. Nutrition is perhaps the most obvious example: we know that inadequate nutrition before birth and in the first years of life can so

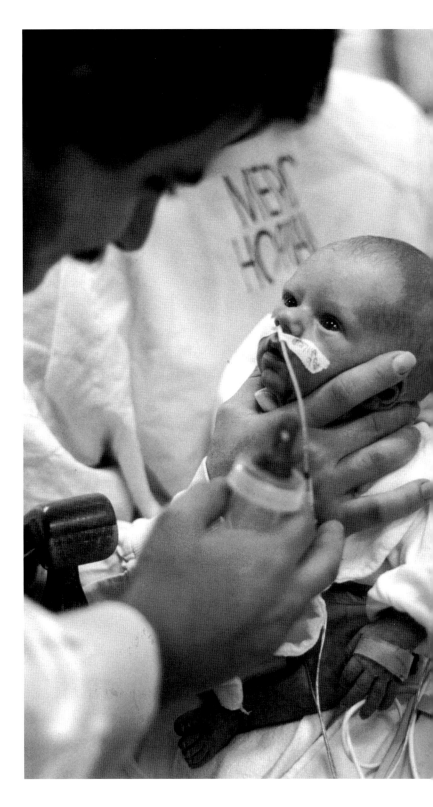

seriously interfere with brain development that it may lead to a host of neurological and behavioral disorders, including learning disabilities and mental retardation.

Beginning in the 1960s, scientists began to demonstrate that the quality and variety of the environment have a direct impact on brain development. Today, researchers around the world are amassing evidence that the role of the environment is even more important than earlier studies had suggested. For example, histological and brain scan studies of animals show changes in brain structure and function as a result of variations in early experience.

These findings are consistent with research in child development that has shown the first eighteen months of life to be an important period of development. Studies of children raised in poor environments—both in this country and elsewhere—show that they have cognitive deficits of substantial magnitude by eighteen months of age and that full reversal of these deficits may not be possible. These studies are based on observational and cognitive assessments; researchers say that neurobiologists using brain scan technologies are on the verge of confirming these findings.[5]

In the meantime, more conventional studies of child development—using cognitive and observational measures—continue to show short- and long-term benefits of an enriched early environment.

- *Third, the influence of early environment on brain development is long lasting.*

We have long suspected that early experience affects later behavior; researchers are now beginning to amass scientific evidence to prove it. One study followed two groups of inner-city children: the first group was exposed, from early infancy, to good nutrition, toys, and playmates; the second was raised in less stimulating settings. The study showed that these factors had a measurable impact on brain function at twelve years of age. The impact by age fifteen appeared to be even greater, suggesting that over time the benefits of early intervention are cumulative.[6]

- *Fourth, the environment affects not only the number of brain cells and number of connections among them, but also the way these connections are "wired."*

Scientists now know that the newborn's brain consists of many more neurons, and more synapses, than it will ever need. Like a sculptor chiseling a form from a block of marble, nature creates the adult brain by eliminating excess neurons and synapses from the very dense immature brain. The result is a more specific and more efficient pattern of connections. This process of refinement continues well into adolescence, but it is most dramatic in the early years of life.

Researchers have not yet isolated the precise factors that control the pruning of excess neurons and synapses, but they know it is not random. Certainly, genetic programming plays a role, but there is growing evidence that the process is guided, to a significant degree, by sensory experience.[7] In other words, the brain uses information about the outside world to design its architecture, particularly in the early years of life.

- *And fifth, we have new scientific evidence for the negative impact of early stress on brain function.*

Researchers have concluded that a child's social environment can quite probably activate hormones in ways that adversely affect brain function, including learning and memory. These effects may be permanent.[8] This research provides a scientific basis for the long-recognized fact that children who have experienced extreme stress in their earliest years are at greater risk for developing a variety of cognitive, behavioral, and emotional difficulties.

All of these findings point to this conclusion: both nature and nurture play a role in human development. We can now say, with far greater confidence than ever before, that the brain responds to experience, particularly in the first years of life. That means that by ensuring a good start in life, we have more opportunity to promote learning and prevent damage than we ever imagined.

Protective Factors in the Early Years

At various points throughout childhood, children are influenced by factors that eventually lead to good or bad outcomes. The "protective factors" that help the child to achieve good outcomes (and avoid bad ones) fall into three broad categories:

- *Temperament and perinatal factors* (such as full-term birth and normal birthweight): having characteristics that attract and encourage caregiving
- *Dependable caregivers:* growing up in a family with one or two dependable adults whose childrearing practices are positive and appropriate
- *Community support:* living in a supportive and safe community

The interaction of these three factors largely influences the direction of children's development. Not surprisingly, it is the inter-action with parents and family members that promotes or hinders the young child's development. Indeed, scientists have found that a major influence in the difference between good and poor outcomes is the quality of parent and family interactions.[9] And clearly the first few years of life establish a trajectory for the parent–child relationship.[10] This period of life appears to be what might be called a "starting point"—a period particularly susceptible to the protective mechanisms of parental and family support.[11] A well-functioning family during the first few years provides a particularly important building block for healthy development.

But what specific parent and family interactions in the first three years help children avoid later psychosocial problems? Primarily, a loving, caring relationship with the child's parents. Infants thrive on one-to-one interactions with parents. The secure attachment that develops between baby and parents is an important achievement for the infant's first year.[12] Sensitive, nurturant parenting is thought to provide infants with a sense of basic trust that allows them to feel confident in exploring the world and forming positive relationships with other children and adults. Conversely, when parents are unable to respond sensitively to their infants' needs because of factors such as marital conflict, depression, or their own history of abuse, the infant develops feelings of helplessness that lead to later difficulties.

Infants' early experiences with adult caregivers also provide the building blocks for intellectual competence and language comprehension. Touching, holding, and rocking a baby, as well as stimulating the child through talking and reading, seem most effective for later development. When parents perform

Being Three: Milestones for Early Growth and Development

For millennia, parents have recognized the newborn's basic need for safety, nourishment, warmth, and nurturing. Now science has added stunning revelations about human development from birth to age three, confirming that parents and other adult caregivers play a critical role in influencing the child's development.

The importance of the first three years of life lies in the pace at which the child is growing and learning. In no other period do such profound changes occur so rapidly: the newborn grows from a completely dependent human being into one who walks, talks, plays, and explores. The three-year-old is learning and, perhaps more important, is learning how to learn.

At age three, children can—given good care and sufficient stimulation—attain a high degree of "competency." Competent three-year-olds are

- Self-confident and trusting
- Intellectually inquisitive
- Able to use language to communicate
- Physically and mentally healthy
- Able to relate well to others
- Empathic toward others

These attributes add up to a good start in life.

Self-Confident and Trusting
Children send signals: Newborns cry and fuss and later smile and frown, one-year-olds point and reach for objects, toddlers ask for help verbally. From adult responses to those signals, infants and toddlers learn

- What they can expect from adults
- That they are important, that their needs and desires matter, and that their actions make a difference
- That they can trust their caregivers, which encourages them to talk, explore, challenge, and learn about the world around them
- That they can succeed
- That adults can be helpful

Intellectually Inquisitive
Even at birth infants show startling intellectual abilities. Newborns touch, see, hear, smell, taste, and make sounds to gather information about their world. Parents and other caregivers exercise enormous influence on intellectual development:

- Babies modify their behaviors in response to sensory information they receive
- Soon, babies use objects that adults give them as tools
- Infants and toddlers imitate adults, pretending to eat dinner, talk on the telephone, play house, read, and care for babies.

Gradually, children embrace the concept of time: infants are locked in the present, but three-year-olds can begin to evoke the past and anticipate the future. Competent three-year-olds can focus on important events and enjoy the challenge of learning new facts, skills, and ways of understanding the world.

Able to Use Language to Communicate
Learning language begins in early mother–child interaction as babies take turns in "conversations" of back-and-forth gazing and gesturing. Through many such exchanges, children learn that

- Their behavior communicates
- They can signal effectively and purposefully, with the expectation of being answered
- Eventually, through language, they can negotiate their own needs while respecting the needs of others, which is the basis of mature friendships and adult relationships

By age three, competent children have replaced crying and smiling with simple, grammatical language. They can verbally

- Exchange ideas, concepts, and feelings with others
- Channel aggression and frustration in healthy ways, learning to substitute words for fists or objects to settle their arguments and vent their feelings

PHYSICALLY AND MENTALLY HEALTHY

Most three-year-old children who are in good health will reach these physical, intellectual, and emotional milestones. Some children, however, are born with disabilities or acquire them through illness or injury. Many such children can, however, with appropriate support and help, move with good speed toward these developmental goals. In addition to biological factors, children's normal growth and development depend on good nutrition, adequate prenatal and comprehensive health care, and a safe home and neighborhood.

By age one, infants triple in weight, double in length, and achieve 80 percent of total brain growth. Adequate nutrition fuels this activity and nourishes brain growth, as well as promoting motor development such as creeping, crawling, and walking. Good health care protects children from disease and corrects problems that may interfere with normal growth. A safe home enables children to grow without the trauma of witnessing or being a victim of violence, which can erase the child's progress toward self-confidence, trust, and curiosity.

The keys to good physical and mental health are

- Preventive services, such as comprehensive prenatal care, immunizations, and screenings to identify and treat visual, hearing, and other problems and to enhance learning and language development
- Adequate nutrition
- Consistent, stimulating, and comforting contact with caring adults
- Homes and communities that are free from violence

ABLE TO RELATE WELL TO OTHERS

From the first moments of life, children have an innate need to relate to other human beings. Parents and other caregivers provide food, warmth, and touching, protecting children from being overwhelmed by information and experiences. They also set limits and teach children to respect the needs and rights of others.

Young children learn from these experiences that they can

- Count on adults to teach them and satisfy their needs
- Make good use of adults when necessary, which offers a beginning to more mature relationships later in life
- Regulate their own impulses and behave in ways that will be acceptable or gratifying to others

EMPATHIC TOWARD OTHERS

Empathy appears to exist in newborns, who make distress cries in response to the cries of other infants. Children

- By age two or three show emotional distress and intervene when others are suffering
- Develop a sense of helping rather than hurting or neglecting, respecting rather than belittling, and supporting and protecting rather than dominating or exploiting others
- By age three have begun to be aware of the thoughts, feelings, and experiences of others

Children's capacity for empathy grows in the context of secure attachments and the example of caring adults: toddlers, for instance, imitate their mothers in helping other children.

This growing sense of connectedness and social responsibility—together with the development of self-confidence, intelligence, language, physical and mental health, social relations, and empathy—makes the first three years of life critical for the individual and for society.

these behaviors in a responsive and attentive manner, they foster their child's early cognitive competence in ways associated with later academic achievement, work performance, and social adaptation.[13]

Parents are also the primary instruments of early socialization. By establishing consistent routines, teaching acceptable behaviors, guiding health habits, and helping children to control disruptive or overly impulsive behavior, parents lay the foundations for the child's capacity to behave in socially acceptable ways.

During the first three years of life, children also learn—or fail to learn—to get along with other people, to resolve disputes peaceably and not through violence, to employ words as tools of learning and persuasion, to be self-confident, and to explore the world without fear. If children are to master these tasks, they need contact with caring adults who are themselves mature and self-controlled and who are knowledgeable about human development. This is the essence of healthy childrearing. A child who learns early is being prepared for life; an individual who must learn these lessons later, as a teenager or adult, faces a daunting task of self-reconstruction.

Just as protective factors help children avoid later problems, so do risk factors lead to later problem behaviors. But the important point about risk factors is that they are often *multiplicative*, not additive, in their effects. Consider, for example, children's risk for social and academic difficulties. When children showed only one risk factor, their outcomes were no worse than those of children showing none of the identified risk factors. But when children had two or more risk factors, they were four times as likely to develop social and academic problems.[14]

An important longitudinal study conducted in Hawaii clearly demonstrates the operation of both risk and protective factors. When children with a variety of perinatal health problems grew up in families that were both poor and dysfunctional, they much more often showed later antisocial behaviors such as truancy and delinquency.[15] Specifically, children who had not developed secure attachments to their parents *and* whose parents had poor parenting skills, high degrees of life stress, and low amounts of social support were much more likely to demonstrate antisocial behaviors.[16] By the same token, various factors protected children from future harm. Children were much less likely to be antisocial or delinquent when their parents showed positive, appropriate child-rearing practices and had high levels of social support.

Policymakers must recognize that it pays to help families increase protective factors in raising their young children. Enhancing parents' social supports, encouraging positive parenting practices, and stimulating the child's cognitive development all appear effective in enabling children to achieve a good start in life.

STRIKING CHANGES IN THE AMERICAN FAMILY

In recent decades, America has been experiencing great change that has contributed to the quiet crisis of our families with infants and toddlers. Two of the most-often-cited causes of this crisis are changing values and the growing economic pressures on families. Examination of the major changes in family relationships and structure provides a basis for understanding how our public and private policies undermine the healthy development of our nation's youngest children.

More Working Mothers

One of the most dramatic changes in the American family is the unprecedented rise in the number of working mothers in the past twenty years. More and more mothers must find an acceptable balance between raising their children and working to produce family income. In the 1970s, few mothers of infants worked outside the home; today, more than half do.[17] The large number of working mothers is a matter of concern because the American workplace is, by and large, not family-friendly, and arrangements for child care for children under three are often hard to find and of poor quality.

Parents increasingly feel the dual stresses of work and family life. On one hand, a growing economy and increased productivity are assumed to hinge, at least in part, on getting more out of those who are working. On the other hand, parents are expected to spend more time with their children, to "get their priorities straight" and value being parents. As a consequence, parents feel overwhelmed. The National Study of the Changing Workforce found that[18]

- Three in ten men and four in ten women "often" or "very often" feel used up at the end of the workday; seven in ten feel that way "some of the time."

- Four in ten men and women "often" or "very often" feel so tired in the morning that it is hard to get up and face another day at work.

Parents are finding that they must devote much more time to earning a living and that they have much less time for their children than their parents had a generation ago. This shift is largely due to the family's economic need to have mothers in the paid labor force.[19] The more hours mothers are employed, the fewer hours they are able to devote to "primary caregiving activities" such as dressing, feeding, playing with, and talking to children. Employed mothers spend an average of six hours each week in primary child care activities—twice as much time as fathers (employed or unemployed) and just under half the average time spent by "nonworking" mothers.[20]

This parental-time deficit also can greatly intensify stress and strain, especially for mothers. After meeting the demands of paid work, mothers more frequently than fathers work a "second shift" at home doing housework and caring for the children. When paid work, housework, and child care are added together, mothers work roughly fifteen hours longer each week than fathers. Not surprisingly, mothers report that they are physically exhausted and emotionally drained.[21]

Many parents report that they are uncomfortable with the loss of family time, the overload and exhaustion that interfere with good parenting. Parents no longer feel willing to "do it all in order to have it all." Both men and women say that they want to work fewer

PARENTS INCREASINGLY FEEL THE DUAL STRESSES OF WORK AND FAMILY LIFE.

hours; neither men nor women want to sacrifice their families to the extent that they have. They do, in fact, value being parents.

Working parents of infants and toddlers need affordable, quality child care; most find it hard to come by. In fact, one quarter of nonworking mothers of young children say that they would seek employment if affordable, quality child care were available.[22]

Empirical studies have established the importance of quality child care for infants and toddlers, but that care is not widely available today in America. Two large, multisite studies have found that the child care they observed, whether center- or family-based, was of such substandard quality that it adversely affected infant and toddler development.[23]

These studies showed that in center-based care, infants and young toddlers spent more than half their time wandering aimlessly; older toddlers were unoccupied a third of the time. Fewer than a third of these children had mastered and were engaged in age-appropriate reciprocal, cooperative, and pretend play with other children. A similar picture emerged in family child care settings. Only 41 percent of providers planned activities for their children: 20 percent of regulated providers, 46 percent of nonregulated providers, and a distressingly high 80 percent of relative providers did not give any thought to what the children were doing during the day. Overall, only 9 percent of family child care and care by relatives was rated as providing good-quality care; 56 percent provided "custodial care," and 35 percent provided care that was completely inadequate. The highest percentage (69 percent) of inadequate care took place, surprisingly, in relatives' homes; and the lowest, 13 percent, in regulated homes. The assumption has been that family child care will be more like a family,

that providers will be more sensitive, and that the children will receive more quality attention and care. The validity of this assumption appears to be in doubt.

More Single-Parent Families

No change in American families should concern this nation more than the skyrocketing number of single-parent families. Since 1950, the percentage of children living in one-parent families has nearly tripled. This tripling is attributable to both increased divorce rates and to the tenfold increase since 1950 in the numbers of births outside marriage.[24] One of four American children now lives in a single-parent home.

But even the term "single-parent family" is a misnomer, since the vast majority of these families—fully 90 percent—are headed by women. These mother-only families often receive little or no help from the child's father: nationwide, only 50 percent of divorced fathers contribute financially to their child's support, and most rarely see their children.[25] As a result, mothers must manage a variety of roles and responsibilities on their own.

The resulting economic deprivation and stress take their toll. Compared to children living in two-parent families, children in single-parent households score worse on measures of health, education, and emotional and behavioral problems.[26] Later on, these children are more likely to drop out of school, to become heads of single-parent families themselves, and to experience a lower socioeconomic status as adults. These conditions—during both early and later childhood—appear to persist even after one adjusts for family income, mother's education, and minority status.[27]

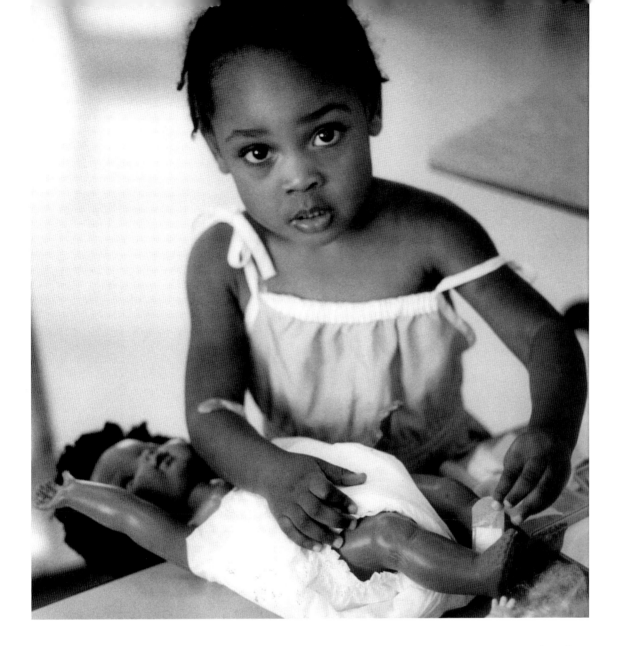

The movement away from the traditional nuclear family is especially pronounced among African Americans, a population that shows declining rates of marriage and remarriage.[28] Many factors contribute to this trend, including the burden of living in poor and unsafe neighborhoods; restrictive Aid to Families with Dependent Children rules that penalize two-parent families; and the obstacles encountered by many African American men as they search for jobs in a difficult economy. For all these reasons, and others, significant percentages of African American children under the age of three are being raised in "single-parent" homes.[29] In reality, many of these children have more than one caregiver. Grandmothers often serve as second mothers to these infants and toddlers; another member of the household—an aunt or a cousin—may become the primary caregiver; or a close friend may take on parenting responsibilities.

This extended notion of family has a positive aspect: it reflects a sense of collective responsibility for children. But it can also add to the stress of already burdened households by disrupting its members' schooling or work lives. When a grandmother leaves a clerical job,

or a sister misses school, to take care of an infant, the long-term consequences to the individual and the household may be devastating.

Another aspect of the changing face of the American family is adolescent pregnancy. More than one million adolescent girls become pregnant in this country every year; approximately half of these pregnancies go to term. Many of these pregnancies are unintended; most often the adolescent parents are unmarried.[30] Compared with older women, most adolescent mothers are neither financially nor emotionally prepared for parenthood. Although certain programs help adolescent mothers,[31] these mothers generally face higher risks of postponed education and of long-term welfare dependency. Children of adolescent parents more often suffer from poor health and poor scholastic performance. For a variety of reasons, at later ages, these children more often become teen parents themselves and consequently have greater difficulty in finding employment and achieving self-sufficiency.[32]

More Family Isolation and Violence

Only a few decades ago, America's families lived in neighborhoods of extended family and friends, in communities served by religious and volunteer organizations. Families sought and found information, advice, help, and emotional (at times, even financial) support from these networks. They depended as well on other community institutions: schools, businesses, parks, recreational facilities, and transportation systems all provided essential supports.

The networks and institutions of the nation's "civil society" seem to have weakened.[33] Most of today's families seem far more isolated from friends, kin, and community life.

BY 1990, FAMILIES WITH CHILDREN UNDER THREE YEARS OF AGE CONSTITUTED THE SINGLE LARGEST GROUP LIVING IN POVERTY IN THE UNITED STATES.

Because people move more often, young families are less likely to live near extended family networks. Greater numbers of working mothers and varied work schedules have interrupted the old rhythms of neighborhood life, making it more difficult for parents to connect with other parents, to support each other, and to build friendships.[34] Few young parents have the time or energy to join volunteer organizations.

When the fabric of community life unravels, parents and their young children suffer. In low-income neighborhoods, fear of crime and violence undermines parents' sense of security and increases their isolation as they struggle to keep their young children safe, healthy, and happy.[35]

Indeed, the escalating rate of violence in many American cities means that families are raising children in what have been described as "inner-city war zones."[36] Evidence from six cities tells the story that even very young children experience extreme violence (assaults, homicides, and rapes) and everyday aggression (shoving, punching, and kicking) as both victims and witnesses.[37] In one survey, 47 percent of mothers reported that their children had heard gunshots in their neighborhood, and one in ten of these young children had witnessed a knifing or shooting before age six. Half of the violence occurred at home and half in the streets.[38]

Although violence is more prevalent in poor inner-city neighborhoods, no city or town is immune. Parents are feeling increasingly unable to protect their children. Nor are traditional protectors—teachers, clergy, youth organization workers, and child care staff members—able to ensure the safety of young children.[39] All too many families feel vulnerable and helpless.

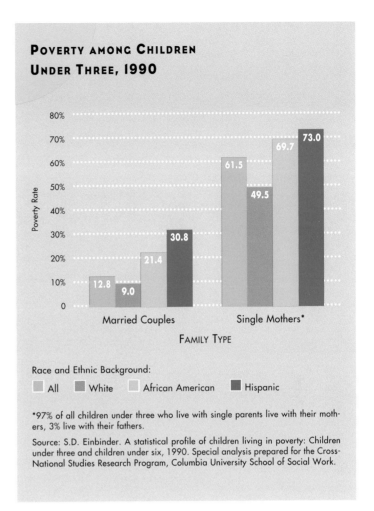

POVERTY AMONG CHILDREN UNDER THREE, 1990

Race and Ethnic Background:
■ All ■ White ■ African American ■ Hispanic

*97% of all children under three who live with single parents live with their mothers, 3% live with their fathers.

Source: S.D. Einbinder. A statistical profile of children living in poverty: Children under three and children under six, 1990. Special analysis prepared for the Cross-National Studies Research Program, Columbia University School of Social Work.

More Young Children in Poverty

By 1990, families with children under three years of age constituted the single largest group living in poverty in the United States: 25 percent of these families fall below the poverty line. The rates are higher still for African American and Hispanic families and single-parent families of young children.[40] Across all ethnic groups and family structures, more children under three live in poverty than do older children, adults, or the elderly.

The poverty rate among young children has risen even though overall American poverty rates are no higher today than they were twenty years ago.[41] This trend contrasts sharply with the status of the elderly. In 1970, one-fourth of those aged sixty-five or older had incomes below the poverty line; today, fewer than an eighth of all elderly people live in poverty,[42] thanks primarily to increased social security and other government benefits. These statistics show that great improvements can be made in the economic conditions of groups of people when social policy directly and forcefully addresses their needs.

MOST POOR CHILDREN UNDER THE AGE OF THREE HAVE AT LEAST ONE WORKING PARENT.

Poverty among young children is a multifaceted problem that is not always eliminated when parents work. In fact, most poor children under the age of three have at least one working parent. But parents' wages are not enough. Housing, transportation, child care, and health care all cost families more today than twenty years ago.[43] In addition, real wages have declined disproportionately for younger as compared to more experienced workers; the decline is even steeper among workers with little education.

Poverty undermines families and the well-being of children in many ways. Poor children are often hungry and inadequately nourished. Many live in overcrowded housing, in unsafe buildings or neighborhoods. Too many are homeless: studies estimate that, of the approximately 100,000 American children who are homeless each night, nearly half are under six years of age.[44]

Such deprivation stacks the deck heavily against poor infants and toddlers. These children more often suffer poor health, maltreatment, and later academic failure.[45] Poverty also seems intertwined with inadequate parenting skills and inconsistent parental behavior. Poor parents—often young, working, raising children alone, and having few supports—simply become overwhelmed, further lessening their infant's or toddler's odds of developing normally.

There are many approaches to improving the income security of families in poverty. Among those that have been implemented are the Family Support Act of 1988, the profamily reforms in the federal tax system (Earned Income Tax Credit, Dependent Care Tax Credit, and personal exemption), as well as federal and state quality education and job training, housing, and neighborhood economic development initiatives. Other means, such as child and family allowances, have been proposed.

Judgments about the specifics of these approaches are beyond the purview of this task force. However, the task force emphasizes that any comprehensive effort to strengthen families must include attention to income security as well as to service and support strategies. The charge of this task force has been to identify strategies that will foster the healthy development of this nation's youngest children. Our recommendations apply to all families with children under three, although most will be particularly helpful to children and families living in poverty.

A NATIONAL INVESTMENT

As the United States approaches the twenty-first century, it faces unprecedented economic challenges at home and abroad. Once the world's innovator and leader in higher education, the United States today is making insufficient investments in its future workforce—its youngest children. In contrast to all the leading industrialized nations, the United States fails to give parents time to be with their newborns, it fails to ensure pre- and postnatal health care for mothers and infants, and it fails to provide adequate child care. The result is significant losses in the quality of its future workforce, citizenry, and parents.

There are, of course, other than economic reasons for protecting young children and their families. Children need to be treasured for their own sake, not merely for what they do for the labor market when they are grown. The task force regards these humanitarian concerns as necessary, wise, and natural to the human species. The issues of "human capital" are real, however, and we now consider them further.

Economists refer to a nation's people as its "human capital." This term encompasses all of our ideas, labor, knowledge, and problem-solving skills—in short, everything used to get the job done. The sum of human capital largely determines a nation's economic performance. In the electronic age, the quality of a nation's human capital is even more important than it was in the industrial age. Producing an automobile requires 40 percent ideas, skills, and knowledge and 60 percent energy and raw materials; producing a computer chip requires 2 percent energy and raw material (mainly sand) and 98 percent ideas, skills, and knowledge.[46]

Increased productivity rates are mainly attributable to improvements in human capital. Since 1929, physical and natural resources (that is, machines and materials) have accounted for 20 percent of productivity increases; 80 percent is attributable to human factors.[47] We can

only expect human factors to become even more important in coming years.

America's business and political leaders are understandably worried about the nation's children and its educational system. Their concern is well founded, but school reform alone is not the answer. A child's capacity to achieve a good education depends in large part on what happens by age three. If the nation is to improve its workforce, it must recognize that, as the 1993 National Education Goals Report notes, "almost half of American babies start life behind and do not get the support needed to catch up."[48] Efforts to raise educational standards and achieve workforce quality goals are unlikely to

AMERICA LAGS BEHIND

The United States:

- Is *not* one of 150 nations that have signed or ratified the UN Convention on the Rights of the Child (Cambodia, Iran, Iraq, Libya, and South Africa have also not signed).
- Is *not* one of 127 nations that permit employees to take paid parental leave after the birth of a baby (as do Canada, France, Germany, and Japan, among others).
- Has a *worse* low-birthweight rate than 30 other nations.
- Has a *smaller* proportion of babies immunized against polio than 16 other nations.
- Has one of the *worst* adolescent pregnancy rates in the developed world—twice high as England and seven times as high as the Netherlands.

Our policies contrast sharply with those of most other industrialized countries, particularly those in Europe. European child care for children under age three varies significantly from country to country, but generally speaking, the Europeans are moving toward paid leaves for new parents and a range of subsidized child care options for toddlers.

Here are some examples of countries that offer job protection and paid leaves to employed parents (usually, but not always, mothers) who have sufficient work histories:

- In Germany, a new parent can receive modest financial support while staying at home for up to one and a half years, or she can work part-time at her previous workplace.
- In France, she can count on modest compensation at home for as long as three years, or she can go back to work and take advantage of subsidized child care.
- In Sweden, she receives full pay while staying at home with a new baby for a year and a half, or she can opt to work part-time for a longer period and receive full pay.
- In Finland, she can stay home until her child is three, knowing that her job (or a comparable job) will be waiting for her when she returns. She receives her full salary for one year and a lesser amount for the next two years. Or she can take advantage of subsidized child care.
- In Austria, she can stay at home throughout her child's first two years, or work part-time until the child's third birthday, while receiving financial support equivalent to the wage of an unskilled worker.

SOURCES:

Children's Defense Fund. *The State of America's Children 1992.* Washington, DC, 1992.

A. Evans and R. B. Friedland. Financing and Delivery of Health Care for Children. Paper prepared for the Advisory Panel on Health Care Financing: Policy and Administrative Choices. Washington, DC: National Academy of Social Insurance, 1993.

S. B. Kamerman. Maternity and parenting benefits: An international overview, pp. 235–275. *In* E. F. Zigler and M. Frank (editors), *The Parental Leave Crisis: Toward a National Policy.* New Haven: Yale University Press, 1988.

S. B. Kamerman and A. J. Kahn (editors). *Child Care, Parental Leave and the Under 3s: Policy Innovation in Europe.* New York: Auburn House, 1991, pp. 16–19.

succeed until this half of America's babies either start life on an equal footing with their peers or receive the support they need to catch up.

Any effort to strengthen the workforce must begin with the family, a key factor in the development of human capital. The family supplies the fundamental learning system to the young child and is the first source of the child's sense of self-worth, motivation, skills, and knowledge.[49] By supporting families during the child's earliest years, society ensures that children will enter school ready to learn, ready, in time, to take their places in the global economy. But the United States ranks low in supporting children under the age of three and their families; other nations, including such high-wage competitors as Germany, invest heavily in early childhood programs.

With regard to young children, America does not put its money where its mouth is: public and private rhetoric strongly supports children and families, but most governmental and business actions do not. Americans view young children as the responsibility of the family, and little economic value is placed on mother' at-home childrearing efforts. Because of this, neither the public nor the private sector has invested much thought or resources in making parents' lives, and the lives of their young children, easier. Still, the stresses imposed by today's demographic, economic, and social trends affect all families, even the

THE COSTS OF SOCIETAL NEGLECT

Each year, American taxpayers reach deep into their pockets to meet the costs, both direct and indirect, of policies that are based on remediation rather than prevention.

- In the six years between 1985 and 1990, estimated public outlays related to teenage childbearing totaled more than $120 billion. More than $48 billion could have been saved if these births had been postponed until the mother was 20 or older.
- Of teens who give birth, 46 percent will go on welfare within four years; of unmarried teens who give birth, 73 percent will be on welfare within four years.
- In 1991, federal and state expenditures for Aid to Families with Dependent Children, the largest entitlement program for poor families, totaled $20 billion plus administrative costs of $2.6 billion.
- In 1991, the estimated annual cost of treating fetal alcohol syndrome was $74.6 million.
- Initial hospital care for each low-birthweight infant averages $20,000. Total lifetime medical costs for a low-birthweight infant average $400,000.

SOURCES:
E. L. Abel and R. J. Sokol. A revised conservative estimate of the incidence of FAS and its economic impact. *Alcoholism: Clinical and Experimental Research* 15:514–524, 1991.

Alan Guttmacher Institute. Washington memo: Prevention strategies discussed for teens at risk—House hearing on adolescent pregnancy focuses on social and economic costs. Washington, DC, December 1992.

Committee on Ways and Means, U.S. House of Representatives. *Overview of Entitlement Programs, 1992 Green Book.* Washington, DC: U.S. Government Printing Office, 1992.

L. V. Klerman, S. S. Brown, and V. L. Poole. The Role of Family planning in Promoting Healthy Child Development. Background paper prepared for the Task Force on Meeting the Needs of Young Children, Carnegie Corporation of New York, February 1993.

U.S. Department of Health and Human Services, Public Health Service. *Healthy People 2000: National Health Promotion and Disease Prevention Objectives.* DHHS Publication Number (PHS) 91-50212. Washington, DC, 1990, p. 191.

most fortunate. And it is not just the families and their children who pay the price, but the nation as a whole. Parents pay the price in anxiety, in lost wages, in missed opportunities. Children pay in poor health, in delayed development, in a clouded future. And the nation pays twice—now, in reduced productivity and increased social disruption, and in the future in a workforce unequal to the demands of the twenty-first century. To avoid these consequences, comprehensive services and supports for families and young children are increasingly necessary.

A FAMILY-CENTERED APPROACH

The quiet crisis of families with children under three requires immediate and far-reaching action. But such action cannot be limited to governmental programs or business initiatives. The problems facing our youngest children

and their families cannot be solved through piecemeal efforts. Americans can work together and invest together confident that they share common values: a strong family, an educated citizenry, a productive workforce, and a competitive and sound economy.

This report argues that America's compassion for its youngest children, measured in investments in high-quality supportive services and opportunities, must no longer be a matter of chance but of sound social policy. Chance is not a force that can sustain children or families, or nations. The task force is convinced that the nation must

- Promote opportunities for responsible parenthood
- Guarantee quality child care choices for children under three
- Ensure good health and protection for infants and toddlers
- Mobilize communities to support young children and their families

These four goals are interrelated, and each addresses a different aspect of the quiet crisis currently growing in this nation. In Part II, the task force proposes workable measures to strengthen families and to foster the healthy development of America's youngest children.

PART II:

STARTING POINTS FOR OUR
YOUNGEST CHILDREN

- WOMEN, CHILDREN, MEN,...
- LIFT UP YOUR HEARTS
- EACH NEW HOUR HOLDS NEW CHANCES
- FOR A NEW BEGINNING
- — MAYA ANGELOU

PROMOTE RESPONSIBLE PARENTHOOD

W e begin with parenting—the most critical starting point. Perhaps nothing we humans do is more relentlessly demanding; nothing calls on a wider range of physical and emotional capacities. To parent a child entails at least two decades of sustained attention; many see it as a lifetime commitment. At the same time, if parents are to acquire the resources they need to support their children, they must work, usually outside the home. Balancing these responsibilities is never easy. For all these reasons, the challenges of parenthood are daunting, but its rewards go to the core of what it means to be human—intimacy, growth, learning, and love.

It is difficult to think of an enterprise that is more deeply private. Childrearing is inseparable from daily domesticity—that messy accumulation of meals and rent payments, laughter and laundry, that fills a home. The kind of care parents give to children, the context they create for their growth, and the framework they create for later learning spring from the rhythms of that life and from the values that give it meaning.

At the same time, it is difficult to imagine an enterprise that has greater impact on public life—on the productivity of our citizenry, the vitality of our culture, and the strength of our public institutions. The time, resources, and energy that parents give to their children influence the children's success as students and their contributions as citizens.[1]

Developing social policy related to early childhood means negotiating the middle ground between these private and public interests. The goal of the task force, in addressing the issue of responsible parenthood, was not to prescribe an approach to childrearing; rather, we sought to identify the kinds of information and services parents need for their own self-directed learning and growth, so that they can make sound choices for their children.

THE CHALLENGES OF PARENTHOOD ARE DAUNTING, BUT ITS REWARDS GO TO THE CORE OF WHAT IT MEANS TO BE HUMAN—INTIMACY, GROWTH, LEARNING, AND LOVE.

We proceed from these assumptions: When women and men make a reasoned commitment to have children, they are more likely to parent well. Their growing children are more likely to meet life with optimism, competence, and compassion. And when women and men are unprepared for the opportunities and responsibilities of parenthood—as is the case all too often in America today—the risks to their children are many and serious.

In the past, parenting skills were often handed down from one generation to the next, as extended families, living in close proximity, shared responsibility for raising children. The enormous changes of this century, increased mobility in particular, have altered the demographics—and consequently the child care arrangements—of many communities. Generally speaking, new mothers and fathers today are less likely to have learned parenting skills first-hand.[2]

THE CHILDREN OF ADOLESCENT PARENTS ARE MORE LIKELY TO SUFFER POOR HEALTH, TO LAG IN SCHOOL, AND TO BECOME TEENAGE PARENTS THEMSELVES.

How then can those who want children prepare themselves for the opportunities and responsibilities of parenthood? How can society help? The task force found that those undertaking parenthood would benefit from education, services, and support in three key areas:

- Planned childbearing
- Prenatal care and support
- Parent education and support

PROMOTE PLANNED CHILDBEARING

One of the most effective ways to promote healthy child development is to encourage women and men to plan childbearing so that it occurs under circumstances that minimize risk for the child. Too often in America, childbearing is not planned. Fully 56 percent of all pregnancies in this country are unintended—one of the highest rates of unintended pregnancy in the industrialized world.[3] Women with unintended pregnancies are less likely than those with planned pregnancies to seek appropriate care for themselves while pregnant, to reduce or quit smoking, or to comply with recommended immunization schedules once the baby is born.[4] The risks of child abuse and neglect, low birthweight, and infant mortality are greater for unplanned children than for those actively planned and welcomed into the world.[5]

The rising rate of teenage pregnancies, 80 percent of which are unplanned,[6] is cause for concern. The risks of unplanned childbearing are compounded in teenagers: Most adolescents are not financially or psychologically ready for parenthood.[7] Adolescent mothers are also at increased risk of long-term welfare dependency.[8] The children of adolescent parents are more likely to suffer poor health, to lag in school, to experience behavior problems, and to become teenage parents themselves.[9] And it is not just a question of the child's welfare: mother, father, and child all fare better if parenthood is postponed to a time when the young people are prepared to accept the responsibilities and opportunities of parenthood.[10]

The costs to society of adolescent pregnancy are immense. In the six years from 1985 to 1990, public outlays related to adolescent childbearing totaled more than $120 billion. It has been estimated that more than $48 billion could have been saved if these births had been postponed until the women were at least twenty years old.[11] In 1990 alone, government spent $25 billion on social, health, and welfare services to families begun by adolescent mothers. By the time babies born to adolescent mothers in 1990 reach voting age, they will have cost the U.S. taxpayer some $7 billion.[12]

The task force concluded that planned childbearing is best achieved when young women and men have access to both family planning services and educational opportunities. Both conditions are essential: educational guidance about planned childbearing works *only* if it is accompanied by a full range of family planning services; likewise, family planning services are better employed when individuals are knowledgeable about their merit and utility.

But improved education about planned childbearing and easier access to family planning services will *not* by themselves solve all of the problems of unintended or at-risk pregnancies. If young women and men are to delay parenthood, they need to believe that other life options more appropriate to their age are available to them.

Those who study poverty in inner-city or rural areas are concerned by the number of very young women—some of them no more than children themselves—who, by becoming mothers, limit their ability to escape degrading conditions. Perhaps if these women and their partners believed that they could make a better life for themselves through quality schooling, job training, and improved economic opportu-

nities, they might delay childbearing. Promoting responsible parenthood means, in part, persuading women and men of reproductive age that they may risk losing opportunities if they do not plan their families wisely.

The task force recommends that efforts to assist women and men in planning for a family must be a part of widely available preventive health services. These services and educational opportunities must be improved, expanded, and adequately financed. Efforts to promote planned childbearing will be most effective when they occur in the context of better life options and increased economic opportunities for both men and women.

Make Family Planning Services Available

Family planning—deciding when to conceive a child, using contraception until that time, and arranging prenatal care—has contributed significantly to the reduction of infant mortality over the past 20 years. On average, women now wait longer than previous generations before having children.[13] Contraception lengthens the interval between births, which in turn contributes to a reduction in low-birth-weight babies.[14] Contraceptive services also lower the number of unintended pregnancies.

Public investment in family planning is known to be cost-effective. According to one set of calculations, every public dollar spent to provide contraceptive services saves an average of $4.40 that would have to be spent on medical care, welfare, and other social services for women who would qualify for such services if they became pregnant.[15] In this way, public investment in family planning saves taxpayers over $3 million each year. This conclusion is based on the following data:

- Each year, about 4.5 million American women now obtain contraceptives from a publicly subsidized source. (They account for about 25 percent of women who use contraceptives.)
- Without public funding for contraception, an average of 1.2 million unintended pregnancies could be expected to occur each year.
- Of these pregnancies, at least 40 percent would probably end in abortion; the other 60 percent—totaling 720,000 pregnancies—would be brought to term.

Increasing the proportion of planned, low-risk births requires a national commitment to making family planning services and information widely and easily available. Additionally, prompt and careful study of innovative ways of making new forms of contraception (for example, Depo-Provera, Norplant, and the "morning-after pill") more readily available must be part of this national commitment. A full range of family planning services must be available so that when birth control efforts fail, access to other services is also possible. These include comprehensive prenatal services and support for every pregnant woman, and in some circumstances access to abortion and adoption services.

Particular attention should be paid to involving men in family planning efforts. Avoiding pregnancy is still perceived by most Americans as "women's work." Pregnancies would undoubtedly be better timed if men understood the importance of planning pregnancies and were willing to communicate with their partners on this issue. The media in general, and male role models in particular, should be urged to help create a climate in which male involvement in family planning is accepted and even encouraged.

The financial benefits of family planning services have been documented, yet the available funds have been drastically reduced. Between 1980 and 1990, total public dollars spent for contraceptive services fell by one-third (from $350 million to $232 million, adjusted for inflation) despite a 15 percent increase (from 34 to 39 million) in the number of women at risk of unintended pregnancy during that same period.[16]

The task force recommends a substantial increase in the resources for family planning services so that they are funded at a level high enough to meet documented needs. Additionally, we recommend that family planning services be included among the preventive health services required as part of a minimum benefits package in health care reform.

Prepare All Young People for Parenthood

Children learn about parenthood and planning for a family from their own parents and families, with the support of schools, religious groups, and community organizations. The quality of this information now ranges from silence, through oblique references to sexuality, to frank, matter-of-fact talk about the medical, financial, and social dimensions of parenthood. With smaller and more isolated families, the opportunities to learn about the joys and responsibilities of parenthood at home have been reduced, and responsibility for "family life education" in American society has shifted primarily to schools. Parents generally support this trend: more than 75 percent of parents feel that schools should play a role in family life education.[17] Although many school districts now offer family life education from kindergarten through grade twelve, the content and quality of the curricula vary considerably.

The task force recommends a substantial expansion of efforts to educate young people about parenthood. Families should be the first source of such education, but schools, places of worship, and community-based youth development organizations also have parts to play. Education about parenthood can begin in elementary school; it should start no later than early adolescence. Such education should cover, in an age-appropriate, culturally sensitive manner, these topics:

- The development of infants, young children, and adolescents, and how parents, families, and communities can meet their needs
- Models of childrearing, parenting skills, and the significance of family composition and environment on child development
- Impact of childbearing and childrearing on the educational and occupational choices of parents, especially mothers

INCREASING THE PROPORTION OF PLANNED, LOW-RISK BIRTHS REQUIRES A NATIONAL COMMITMENT TO MAKING FAMILY PLANNING SERVICES AND INFORMATION WIDELY AND EASILY AVAILABLE.

Preparing Young People for Responsible Parenthood

Early adolescence provides unprecedented opportunities for educators and health professionals to capitalize on young people's natural curiosity about bodily changes to promote healthier lifestyles that will have long-lasting benefits. By the same token, it is during adolescence that this same curiosity may lead young people to engage in self-damaging behaviors that may shorten life or impair its quality. For example, more and more adolescents are becoming sexually active at an earlier age, risking pregnancy, sexually transmitted diseases, a high miscarriage and abortion rate, and poor pregnancy outcomes such as low-birthweight babies. To be healthy, young people need both critical information and access to health services. Two promising directions are described below.

Comprehensive Human Biology Curriculum

- A comprehensive human biology curriculum has been developed by educators at Stanford University. The Human Biology Middle Grades Life Science Project has developed a two-year curriculum that should help adolescents understand and cope with the social, behavioral, and health problems they encounter. The curriculum covers adolescent development and physiology, genetics, and environmental science. Units such as "Your Community Culture," "Youth and Family," and "Become an Adult" help students to learn about human development and to develop the responsible attitudes and behaviors that are the foundations of effective parenthood.

Comprehensive Family Life Education and Health Services

- A growing number of middle and high schools, with parental approval, are offering adolescents a good start toward responsible parenthood by combining family life education with the needed health services and supports to avoid early childbearing. Comprehensive school health services help adolescents to delay sexual activity, offer knowledge about effective methods of pregnancy and disease prevention, including abstinence and contraception, and provide prenatal health services to adolescents who do become pregnant; the centers also provide preventive health services such as immunizations. Young people find these health centers responsive, convenient, and economical.

Together, these approaches provide a comprehensive strategy that more schools should adopt.

- Human reproduction, including the role of overall health in reproductive outcomes; methods of birth control, including abstinence; and the importance of health protection and promotion in the prenatal period
- The causes of sexually transmitted diseases and ways of avoiding them
- The effect of behavioral and environmental threats (including stress, poor nutrition, violence, and substance abuse) on the health of pregnant women and of children and families
- The availability of social services and other neighborhood supports, ranging from family planning and early intervention services for families at risk to Head Start programs and community health and social services

Religious groups, community programs, and the media can deliver helpful and healthy messages that complement those that young people receive at home and school. These messages must emphasize that all children need committed parents and families. Young men in particular must understand their responsibilities as fathers.

Encourage Pre-conception Care

Research confirms the lessons of common sense: it is unwise to isolate planning for a family from general health and social services. Evidence points increasingly to the importance of a woman's overall health status to her reproductive life. Indeed, all aspects of a woman's life affect the child she carries.

A landmark U.S. Public Health Service report observed that pre-conception diagnosis and treatment of medical and psychosocial risks can eliminate or reduce hazards to mother and child and are more likely to be effective because they can be initiated without harm to any fetus. "For example, preexisting illness such as diabetes or hypertension should be adequately treated or controlled, and behavior such as smoking, drinking, or using illicit drugs should be modified or eliminated before pregnancy onset," the report said. "Preconception identification of women with any kind of medical illness or unhealthy behaviors provides the opportunity for appropriate treatment, pregnancy planning, early entry into prenatal care, or recommendations for avoidance of pregnancy."[18]

Women who want children should have a medical checkup before conception. Too often, women are several months pregnant before seeking medical advice, and the delay may compromise healthy fetal development.[19]

Because the greatest sensitivity to environmental factors occurs between 17 and 56 days after conception, this period is especially important.[20] A woman whose pregnancy is unplanned is at particularly high risk, as are women who are taking prescription medications or abusing alcohol or drugs. These women may be risking serious damage to the embryo and fetus without knowing it; a checkup before conception will give them the opportunity to change their use of these substances in time to avoid potential damage to the fetus.[21]

Many substances adversely affect fetal development. Fetal alcohol syndrome, the most serious consequence of heavy drinking in pregnancy, may cause learning disabilities and mental retardation in the child[22]; smoking, poor nutrition, and the use of other drugs worsen the effects of alcohol. These substances are particularly harmful to the fetal brain, which experiences the fastest growth of any organ during pregnancy.[23] Other substances are also harmful: exposure to lead early in fetal life, for example, can cause irreversible damage to the developing central nervous system, and even exposure to dental and other x-rays can harm a fetus.

What a woman does *not* consume is also important. For example, folic acid deficiency in the diet of pregnant women may cause spinal column defects in the child. A chronically malnourished woman is apt to be in relatively poor physical condition before and during pregnancy. Compared to a well-nourished woman, she is less likely to be able to fight off infections and more likely to deliver prematurely a low-birthweight baby with physical, behavioral, and intellectual difficulties.[24]

Women and men need to know these facts. The task force concurs with the Public Health Service in recommending that, by the year 2000, all parents-to-be make a pre-conception health visit that would cover nutrition, contraception, and healthy behaviors in a comprehensive way.[25]

ENSURE COMPREHENSIVE PRENATAL CARE AND SUPPORT

Pregnancy provides one of life's "teachable moments." A pregnant woman is likely to be highly receptive to information about her own health care, that of her family, and especially that of her soon-to-arrive child. The task force recommends that prenatal care be broadly defined to include at least four components:

- Early and continuing risk assessment
- Health education and promotion
- Medical and social support services
- Medical treatment for at-risk conditions

In the best settings, prenatal care is carefully tailored to the needs, preferences, and risk profile of the individual woman. It may include HIV screening: approximately 30 percent of infants born to women infected with HIV (Human Immunodeficiency Virus) will be HIV-infected and will have significant health problems.[26] Doctors and nurse–midwives attend not only to medical needs, but also to each woman's nutritional and psychological needs. They advise pregnant women against smoking, substance abuse, environmental toxins, and excessive stress. They are alert to signs of domestic violence. Sensitive physicians also attempt to diagnose and treat depression: depressed pregnant women are more likely to jeopardize their own and their babies' health through smoking, substance abuse, and poor nutrition.[27]

More than physical health is at stake during the prenatal period. An infant's capacity for learning in the critical years following birth is intimately tied to brain development *in utero* (see Part I), and thus to the prenatal environment that the mother provides. During pregnancy, chemical, viral, or bacterial agents may cross the placental barrier and cause abnormalities in the developing embryo or fetus, particularly the developing brain. Children exposed to drugs *in utero* are prone to learning difficulties, attention deficits, and hyperactivity as well as to behavioral and psychosocial problems.[28]

The benefits of prenatal care, particularly in the first trimester, have been repeatedly documented: women who receive a full course of such care stand a much better chance of delivering healthy, full-term, normal-weight babies than women who do not. Low-birthweight infants (2500 grams or less) are significantly more likely than normal-birthweight infants to have neurodevelopmental handicaps.[29] Centers that follow low-birthweight infants report rates of learning difficulties running as high as 40 to 45 percent.[30] Further, low-birthweight and premature babies are more likely to have congenital anomalies and more frequent respiratory tract infections. Over 40 percent of these infants are rehospitalized more than once in their first year of life.[31]

In short, we have overwhelming evidence that prenatal care is crucial to the health and well-being of our youngest children. But the

WE HAVE OVERWHELMING EVIDENCE THAT PRENATAL CARE IS CRUCIAL TO THE HEALTH AND WELL-BEING OF OUR YOUNGEST CHILDREN. BUT THE EVIDENCE IS ALSO MOUNTING THAT MILLIONS OF AMERICAN CHILDREN ARE COMING INTO THE WORLD WITHOUT BENEFIT OF THIS CARE.

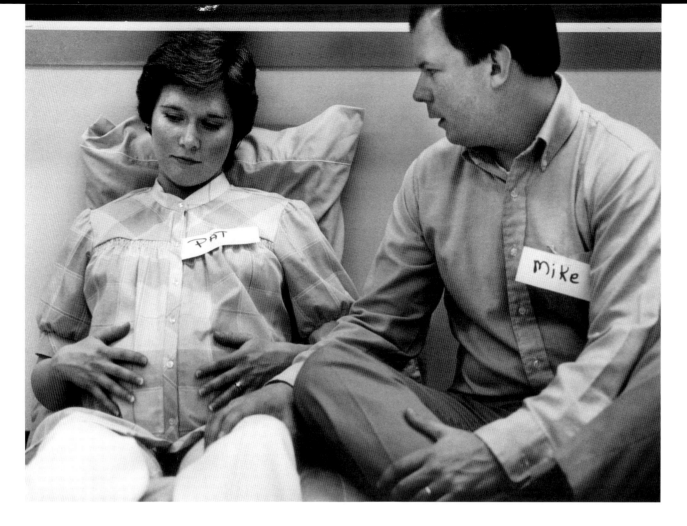

evidence is also mounting that millions of American children are coming into the world without benefit of this care, and their numbers are increasing[32]:

- About one-fourth of pregnant women do not receive the recommended level of prenatal care.
- The percentage of pregnant women who receive virtually no prenatal care (no more than a visit or two in the last few weeks of pregnancy) has increased in recent years.
- Mothers are less likely to obtain adequate or prompt prenatal care if they are young, poor, unmarried, relatively uneducated, uninsured, or living in inner cities or rural areas.

There are some encouraging signs: since the 1980s, the proportion of African American and Native American women who obtained early prenatal care rose from about 40 percent to 60 percent.

Women with unintended pregnancies tend to obtain prenatal care later than those with intended pregnancies. Women who do not expect to conceive may be less aware of the signs and symptoms of pregnancy and therefore may recognize the pregnancy later. Those who view their pregnancy negatively may delay prenatal care while deciding whether to seek abortion. Moreover, an unplanned pregnancy is likely to evoke ambivalent feelings that may result in late or sporadic care. Here again, one sees the links among family planning, intended pregnancy, early prenatal care, and healthy infants.

The task force concurs that all pregnant women must be drawn into comprehensive prenatal care early in pregnancy. This requires

PRENATAL CARE: THE KEY TO A HEALTHY BABY

Obtaining early and comprehensive prenatal care is the best thing a woman can do to have a healthy baby. Yet the importance of prenatal care in reducing infant mortality and low-birthweight babies is not always understood by the general public, nor are services readily available to all pregnant women.

Through the Southern Regional Project on Infant Mortality, many states in the South are developing innovative and effective strategies to increase the availability and use of prenatal care.

SOUTH CAROLINA MOUNTS A PUBLIC AWARENESS CAMPAIGN

South Carolina's "Caring for Tomorrow's Children" program combines a media campaign, a statewide hotline, and an incentive program to spread the message about the importance of prenatal care.

- The media component brings its message to the public through posters, billboards, brochures, and television and radio announcements.
- The campaign links pregnant women to the statewide information and referral hotline to help them make their first prenatal care appointments.
- The incentive program encourages women to begin prenatal care as early as possible by offering coupons redeemable for services and products such as diapers and bibs. Coupons are validated by the woman's prenatal care provider at each appointment.

LOUISIANA AND GEORGIA HELP REDUCE THE SHORTAGE OF PRENATAL CARE PROVIDERS

In 1990 the Louisiana legislature passed the Health Care Access Act. The act requires medical, nursing, and allied health schools to adopt programs and policies that will result in more perinatal health care providers returning to rural and other underserved areas. State medical school admissions policies must ensure that students from rural and underserved areas make up half of each first-year class. The act also encourages support and relief services for overworked health care professionals who practice in medically underserved areas of the state.

In 1986 Georgia developed the Nurse Midwifery Project to recruit certified nurse–midwives for underserved areas of the state. Within three years, 3,318 women and their infants received prenatal and delivery services through the project, at a total cost of only $1.4 million. The project has been successful in lowering infant mortality rates: The state's infant mortality rate in 1988 was 12 per thousand; for infants whose mothers received prenatal and delivery services from the project's certified nurse–midwives the rate was 8.2.

THE DISTRICT OF COLUMBIA EMPLOYS A MATERNITY OUTREACH MOBILE VAN

The District of Columbia's Department of Health and Human Services employs an outreach worker to drive a van through the city's neighborhoods and transport pregnant women who have not yet obtained prenatal care to an appropriate provider. Each week the van travels to those areas of the city with the highest infant mortality and morbidity rates. The outreach worker talks to women in the neighborhoods, distributes perinatal health care information, and offers advice on good prenatal health care habits and nutrition. The person-to-person contact enables the outreach worker to build relationships with the local people, who often help her identify women who are in need of transportation and referral assistance.

the intensification of national, state, and local efforts to improve the availability and use of prenatal services. Specifically we recommend the removal of the barriers that now stop women from receiving comprehensive prenatal care, including inadequate financing and the absence of local services, particularly in inner-city and isolated rural areas. Cultural and language barriers and the lack of child care, transportation, and translation services also keep many women from receiving prenatal care. A woman's fears about being pregnant or her lack of understanding of the importance of care are

Improving Life Outcomes for Adolescent Mothers and Their Children

Many communities are taking a two-generation approach to changing life outcomes for the better, by offering programs that serve both mothers and their babies. The services may be offered through community settings such as schools, health facilities, or neighborhood family-child centers. When programs are well-designed, beginning during pregnancy and continuing after the baby is born, outcomes are encouraging, especially for adolescent mothers and their children.

Visiting Nurses
One highly promising strategy to reach mothers and children is through home visits. Frequent home visits by nurses during pregnancy and the first two years of the child's life have been shown to reduce many of the health and social problems associated with childbearing among adolescent, unmarried, and low-income mothers.

Pregnant women who participated in the Prenatal and Infancy Home Visiting Program in Elmira, New York, for example, cut down on cigarettes and improved their diets, experienced greater informal social support, and made better use of childbirth education and the Women, Infants, and Children (WIC) nutritional supplementation program. These women also had 75 percent fewer preterm deliveries. Babies born to young adolescents who had been visited by nurses weighed more on average than babies of young mothers who had not been visited. Among mothers who were poor, unmarried, and adolescent, a 75 percent reduction in cases of child abuse and neglect was observed. Children who were visited by nurses had 32 percent fewer emergency room visits during the second year of life, and low-income, unmarried women who

were visited participated in the workforce 80 percent more and bore 43 percent fewer subsequent children than those provided with less comprehensive services.

School-Based Programs
Another promising way to improve outcomes for young mothers and their babies is by using comprehensive school-based programs. The Polly T. McCabe Center in New Haven, Connecticut, for example, is a short-term public school for pregnant students and new mothers, who otherwise might be forced to drop out of school. In addition to education, the center offers social and medical services. It features small class sizes, high-quality individually paced instruction, personalized guidance, and mentoring. Students are encouraged to consider long-term life options as they make progress toward completing their high school education. The goal of the program is to help the students plan for eventual self-sufficiency—including delaying subsequent childbearing, which has been shown to be a major predictor of greater success in life.

The most surprising finding of this program's evaluation was that students who remained seven weeks or longer postnatally were almost three time less likely to deliver a new baby within the next two years than students who left McCabe sooner. Five years after the birth of their first child, those same students still showed the effects of their stay at McCabe: 70 percent of the short-stay mothers had delivered one or more children, while only 45 percent of those who stayed seven weeks or more had done so.

also barriers to seeking out prenatal care. Clinicians, educators, and social workers must help pregnant women understand how important prenatal care is to their own and their children's well-being.

Of all of these barriers, money is probably the most important for most women. Health care financing systems are badly needed to sup-

port continuity among prenatal, delivery, and postpartum care. Financing for prenatal care is often spotty; it sometimes does not cover delivery; and it often fails to provide even rudimentary follow-up care to new mothers who need extra support and education.

We have ample evidence that investments in prenatal care pay off: For example, the Office of Technology Assessment concluded in 1988 that prenatal care helps decrease the incidence of low-birthweight infants. For every instance of low-birthweight averted by earlier or more frequent prenatal care, the U.S. health care system saves between $14,000 and $30,000 in newborn hospitalization, rehospitalization in the first year, and long-term health care costs.[33]

The task force recommends that all pregnant women have universal access to comprehensive prenatal care as a core component of any health care reform package that this nation adopts. It would be a wise and cost-effective investment to have pregnant women phased in first, because of their overrepresentation among the uninsured and because a healthy start in a child's life holds the promise of a lifetime of productivity.

PROVIDE OPPORTUNITIES FOR PARENT EDUCATION AND SUPPORT

No job is more important to our nation's future than that of a parent, and no job is more challenging. But while society readily acknowledges the value of job training in other areas, it tends to act as if parenting skills should come naturally. Too often, policymakers base decisions on this assumption, overlooking their own experience, both as parents and as children. For most parents, raising children is a trial-and-error process marked by countless frustrations. Parents across all social and economic strata enter parenthood wanting to do a good job, but they frequently have limited experience or knowledge about raising children. They are often reluctant to admit that they might benefit from learning more about children and parenting. Yet, effective parent education and support can build on families' strengths so that parents feel more knowledgeable, more confident, and more valued.

The task force notes that many—perhaps most—parents could benefit from parent education and support, parent-to-parent support, or both. This is especially true for parents of infants and toddlers. Even in the best of circumstances, the newness of the parental role, coupled with the child's rapid physical, intellectual, and emotional development, make the parents' job demanding and at times overwhelming. As a result, parent education and support programs have appeared, ranging from grassroots, community-based efforts staffed with volunteers (for example, the pioneering Family Focus Program begun in Evanston, Illinois), to statewide programs, such as those in Kentucky, Missouri, and Minnesota, that are available on a universal and voluntary basis.

These initiatives are found under many names in different localities; moreover, the distinctions remain blurred between parent education and family support. Operationally, the two go hand in hand. In some instances, a family support program may be mostly a parent education and emotional support program; elsewhere, it may include services such as literacy classes or job training. Most programs have abandoned a one-size-fits-all approach and recognize that the critical ingredient is responsiveness to family strengths and needs.

Pregnancy and the immediate postpartum period also offer excellent opportunities to provide new mothers with important health education. Sensitive practitioners can talk with mothers about the importance of breast-feeding, nutrition, and injury prevention; can refer them to helpful community services; and can detect early signs of child abuse. Follow-up care for mothers in high-risk settings (for example, very young single mothers) is especially important. In poor communities, young parents need a dependable person who can provide social support through the months of pregnancy and beyond.

Key Elements of Supportive Parent Education

Families vary tremendously in their structure, values, needs, and resources, as well as in their ability to seek and use parent education and support. Still, certain key elements define successful parent education. Successful programs

- Establish and maintain an ongoing relationship with parents
- Are geared to the strengths, styles, and needs of individual families
- Increase understanding of child development and parent–child relationships
- Provide models of parenting
- Teach new parenting skills
- Provide a network of social support with other parents
- Facilitate access to community resources

Two Programs that Improve Parents' Childrearing Skills

Imaginative programs in Oregon and Texas demonstrate that parent education and support can be offered to the general population as well as to specific groups and can improve parents' childrearing skills.

Oregon — Birth to Three

Since 1978, the nonprofit organization Birth To Three has brought new parents in Eugene, Oregon, together to share experiences, study early child development, form a support network, and learn about community resources. Programs are community- or school-based and are run by professional staff members assisted by volunteers.

More than 10,000 families have benefited from this program, which is offered to all families—there are groups for single parents, working parents, and parents with multiple births. A program aimed at pregnant teenagers and teenage parents includes weekly group meetings, home visits, crisis assistance, and life-skills training. All parents have access to a resource hotline, newsletter, and posters; a weekly parenting column also appears in the local newspaper.

Texas — Avance

A widely acclaimed family support and education program begun in Texas in 1973 serves Mexican American families. Each year Avance serves 2,000 families with young children in Houston, San Antonio, and the Rio Grande Valley. Avance operates in public housing centers, in elementary schools, and through its family service centers. Its Parent–Child Education Program conducts home visits by trained staff members (many of them former participants), presents weekly classes on child growth and development, and disseminates information about community services, English classes, and high school and employment preparation courses.

Avance provides free child care so that mothers can attend classes; when their children are older, some mothers serve as volunteer aides at the child care center, thus learning more about child development. Avance staff members, most of whom have some college education in relevant disciplines, emphasize individual attention to the child and support for the mother. Avance also involves fathers: staff encourage fathers to participate at the centers and connect fathers with job training initiatives, parenting education, and social support networks.

Evaluations show that Avance programs improved families' ability to provide an emotionally stimulating and nurturing environment for their young children, positively influenced mothers' childrearing attitudes and knowledge, and expanded mothers' use of community resources.

Good parent education and support programs share many goals. They seek to respond to family strengths and needs, to improve parental attitudes and behavior toward the child, and to heighten the child's chances of becoming a healthy and resilient adult. Beyond that, great variation exists.

The task force finds that parent education and support can be effective. A variety of programs have been found to have consistent and persistent influence on both parental behavior and the intellectual development of the young children.[34] Researchers have also found secondary benefits: for example, mothers who have taken part in parent education programs provide more age-appropriate toys and spend more time reading to their young children than do mothers who have not. Modest benefits also accrue to the parents: compared with other mothers, for example, program participants express more confidence and satisfaction with parenting. These are welcome results, because improved interactions within the family system may have a substantial and lasting influence on the family environment and the child's development.

Parent education and support programs should match family strengths and needs. For example:

- Parents who lack transportation or who have other young children at home may benefit more from an individualized, home-based approach; more socially oriented parents, including adolescents, might prefer peer discussion groups.

- Parents of infants may find a home-based approach more effective; as their babies become toddlers, they may prefer a combination of a play group and group discussion.

- Working parents might find it more sensible to have parent education and support tied to a child care program.

- Parents of children with special needs may find it helpful to participate in groups headed by other experienced parents. Such parent-to-parent support networks have been established in virtually every state.

- Parents living in rural areas, where groups might be more difficult to assemble, might seek advice and support from professionals and other parents via computer networks or teleconferencing.

The task force recognizes that families with high levels of stress and severe economic hardship have urgent needs that clearly cannot be met through education alone. For these families, parent education will do little good unless it is combined with substantive and sustained support. As a task force member said, "A few parent education classes in the public housing projects and other places where low income people are congregated will not eliminate child abuse and other forms of violence, get children ready for school, instill responsibility, conscience and good values in young children." Parent education opens the door, but it must be linked to ongoing family support. However, the desire of families to take good care of their infants and toddlers can provide an opportunity to address other issues.

The task force concluded that to serve these families, parent education and support programs must be built into a coordinated array of services such as health care, child care, literacy classes, and job training. Some communities have formed coalitions to coordinate services. These coalitions have been able to generate public support and local funding, utilize local resources, and identify and expand promising new programs; they also are able to match families with suitable programs. Parent education and support programs appear to have come to be accepted as one of the basic elements of an integrated approach to supporting families.

Many parent education and support programs enthusiastically recruit local community members as key staff contacts with parents. This approach has the advantages of providing training and employment for members of the community, drawing on the insights of people who have lived in similar social situations, and avoiding disparities in culture, language and values between clients and practitioners.[35]

FAMILIES WITH HIGH LEVELS OF STRESS AND SEVERE ECONOMIC HARDSHIP HAVE URGENT NEEDS THAT CLEARLY CANNOT BE MET THROUGH EDUCATION ALONE.

How States Can Support
Parenting Education

State initiation and financing of family support programs is still relatively new. Many states have developed successful programs designed to meet various needs: to prepare children for school (Missouri), to teach parenting techniques (Minnesota), to improve family literacy (Kentucky), and to support teenage parents (Maryland).

Missouri's Parents as Teachers (PAT) program sends certified parent educators to visit expectant families at home and teach them how to be "their child's first teacher." PAT staff members set up group meetings for parents, screen children for early detection of problems, and link parents with other community resources, such as child care, health, and social services. Because this state-legislated program crosses all socioeconomic and educational boundaries, it attracts both high-risk families and those who need less intensive services and supports. Evaluations show that PAT children score well above national norms on measures of school-related achievement and that parents like the program. PAT had grown from four pilot sites in Missouri in 1981 to 1,233 programs in forty-two states, the District of Columbia, and four foreign countries by late 1993.

Minnesota's Early Childhood Family Education program is a statewide, state-funded effort operating in more than 300 school districts. It offers child development information and parenting techniques, encourages healthy communication between parent and child, and promotes positive parental attitudes. The program is open to all families with children from birth to kindergarten. Parents and children spend an average of two hours a week at the center: parents spend time with their children and talk with other parents while their children, overseen by trained early childhood educators, engage in discovery and cooperative play, learn to separate from parents, and develop cognitive and motor skills. Centers employ licensed early childhood and parent educators, as well as aides and volunteers from local communities.

Kentucky enacted the Kentucky Education Reform Act of 1990 to reduce barriers to learning. Family Resource Centers (for families with children up to age five) operate out of elementary schools. Within two years, 223 centers, funded through a competitive grant process, opened throughout the state; a total of 378 centers now serve 57 percent of the state's families with children under the age of five. The Family Resource Centers offer before- and after-school child care, child development education for pregnant women and mothers, literacy training for mothers who are earning their GED, training and supervision for child care providers, and health and social services referrals. The program receives local and private funding.

Maryland's Friends of the Family is a statewide network of family support centers administered by an independent agency established with state assistance in 1985 to address high rates of teenage pregnancy and child abuse and neglect. Today, this public–private agency oversees thirteen family support centers that primarily serve mothers younger than twenty-five with children younger than three. All centers provide social support services, assistance in child development and parenting education, and assistance for those completing their GED. The centers emphasize close community ties through their policy advisory boards, which include parents, community leaders, and social service agency representatives. They also find hard-to-reach families and provide supplementary services such as child care and transportation.

For example, South Carolina's Resource Mothers home visiting program links pregnant adolescents with "resource mothers"—experienced mothers who live nearby. They have successfully raised their own children and can help new mothers learn the adaptive skills they urgently need; they can also help them gain access to community resources. Just as importantly, resources mothers offer sympathetic and sustained attention.[36] Such prenatal and postpartum home visiting services have been shown to improve the health of babies, reduce child abuse, and save money.[37]

Some experts have concluded, however, that the most successful programs depend on more highly trained professionals who can apply general principles to different family types and cultures.[38] Debate about staffing exists, but there is agreement that a key component for both professionals and paraprofessionals is the individual's level of training. A number of universities are now engaged in research and program development focused on parent education and support.

Shift in Thinking Needed

The task force recommends that parent education and support be available on a voluntary basis to all parents with children under age three. It is a preventive strategy that can strengthen all families, particularly those with infants and toddlers, thus improving conditions in which very young children are raised. It is often said that children are our most valuable natural resource, but children do not come without families. It is time to develop strategies to conserve and nurture the family environment of our future generations. A commitment to providing parent education and support programs in every American community could signal a shift in national thinking from the current state of supporting specific individuals and families to valuing families within the community.

Policymakers and program administrators recognize the need for such programs along with other services that benefit families with young children. Innovative state legislation, such as Missouri's Parents As Teachers Education Act of 1981, and statewide initiatives, such as those launched in Minnesota and Kentucky—open the way to support families. The task force encourages all states and communities to use funds from existing state and federal sources and from new sources, such as the federal Family Preservation and Support Service Program, to initiate and expand community-based parent education and support programs for families with infants and toddlers.

CHILDREN ARE OUR MOST VALUABLE NATURAL RESOURCE, BUT CHILDREN DO NOT COME WITHOUT FAMILIES. IT IS TIME TO DEVELOP STRATEGIES TO CONSERVE AND NURTURE THE FAMILY ENVIRONMENT OF OUR FUTURE GENERATIONS.

GUARANTEE QUALITY CHILD CARE CHOICES

O ver the past three decades, American family life has changed dramatically, forcing a reconsideration of family policy. The most significant change has been the increasing numbers of mothers in the workforce. Whereas only 17 percent of mothers of one-year-olds worked full-time or part-time in 1965, fully 53 percent were in the labor force in 1991. More than five million infants and toddlers are now in the care of other adults while their parents work.[1] In a very real sense, both parents and child care providers are jointly raising many of this nation's youngest children.

How well is the current system of child care meeting the needs of our youngest children and their families? In some well-run settings, competent child care providers attend to small numbers of children, and infants and toddlers experience a happy and stimulating day. But in many other settings, five, six, or even seven infants are cared for by one well-meaning provider. At any one time, this caregiver can console, nurture, pick up, and talk to only one or two babies; the other babies are ignored. Children (and adults) in these settings— which probably constitute the majority—are overstressed and unhappy.

Yet many parents of infants and toddlers have few child care choices. They would like to stay home longer after their baby is born, but someone must pay the bills. Faced with the challenge of arranging child care for the first time, most parents feel scared, guilty, and terribly alone. Most are concerned about what will happen when they are not with their baby; they seek a provider who they think will give the baby the kind of care and consistency they would if they were at home. Unfortunately, many parents are forced to "make do"—to accept care that is safe and affordable but that falls short of the quality they would like for their young child. Many find themselves searching again and again for new arrangements as their initial "choices" prove unreliable and unstable. The disruption to the child, the family, and the parents' working life is immense and costly.

MORE THAN 5 MILLION INFANTS AND TODDLERS ARE NOW IN THE CARE OF OTHER ADULTS WHILE THEIR PARENTS WORK.

43

THE SEARCH FOR CHILD CARE

Unpaid bills have piled up, helpful in-laws have departed, and the young parents of a newborn now face the challenge of finding child care. The father is already back at work and, six months after delivering, the mother must also earn money. She lost her job when she left to have the baby.

The couple agonizes over whether the mother is leaving the child too soon, whether they can find care as good as they themselves provide, whether they can find *any* acceptable care. They have talked with friends and family, done their reading, and they know that the arrangement they make will influence the healthy development of their child.

Friends warn of problems; a few say, "You just have to be lucky." They visit family child care settings in the neighborhood and child care centers. The family child care home they liked had no openings, and in the other, the parents agreed, the provider was already caring for too many young children—three infants and two four-year-olds. In one center they are appalled to see a worker feeding five babies, lined up in five highchairs, from one bowl of cereal. Other centers are too expensive or too far away. Ideally, the mother would like to find both work and child care with an employer who provides a quality center. Her inquiries turn up no such opportunity.

Their only choice may be the one affordable center in their area that has an opening: the center where the babies were lined up in the highchairs.

As a result of this child care crisis, many of our youngest children suffer. They miss important early experiences that are necessary to develop healthy intellectual and social capacities. It is no wonder that parents are concerned. Their children's well-being is jeopardized by

- Poor-quality care
- Lack of affordable care
- High turnover among providers due to inadequate compensation and working conditions
- Weak consumer protection
- A fragmented system of delivery

This chapter offers strong evidence that our society has an important responsibility to provide all parents who need it with quality, affordable child care. The costs of providing such care will be significant, but the costs of ignoring the growing crisis in child care quality are even higher.

The task force strongly recommends that our nation make the availability of quality child care choices to all parents of infants and toddlers a high priority. Such availability fosters the healthy growth and development of children, their readiness for school, and eventually their productivity as members of the workforce.

Parents need options about when to begin child care, and they need child care arrangements that are high-quality, accessible, and affordable. These options include a continuum of parental and nonparental forms of care throughout the first three years. This nation will ensure that parents have genuine choices about the care of their young children when we

- Improve parental leave benefits
- Ensure quality child care for infants and toddlers
- Provide parents with affordable child care options
- Develop networks of family-centered child care programs for infants and toddlers

IMPROVE PARENTAL LEAVE BENEFITS

Infants' early experiences are critical to their healthy development. Experts can now substantiate the benefits of allowing ample time for the mother to recover from childbirth and for the parents to be with their new baby during the first months of life.[2] Most physicians recommend at least six to eight weeks away from work for full medical recovery from

rth. Infants have a
...n parents are able to
...early months. Breast-
...re offer protection
...infant has developed

...ogether is critically
...ip between infants
...re very sensitive to
...he adults who care
...consistent parental
...st months allows
...aby form secure,
...and other family
...responsiveness is
...s become confi-
...learn that their
...t they do makes
...is necessary for
...nent through-

...need time to
...an infant is a
...s life. Parents
...ir infants, to
...patterns, and
...rs learn to
...through these earliest
interactions, and early success helps parents to become confident in their new roles. Such success is especially difficult to achieve when both parents have demanding work schedules. When adequate parental leave benefits enable infants and parents to have sufficient time together, everyone profits.

When new mothers are surveyed on how long a parental leave they would prefer, they say six months. They want time to get to know the baby; time to adjust to the baby's schedule,

to find quality child care, and to phase in their return to work.[3] Experts generally recommend a four- to six-month parental leave as critical to fostering healthy infant development.[4]

As employment rates have soared among women with young children, public support has grown for parental leave policies, and it has gradually influenced many sectors of our

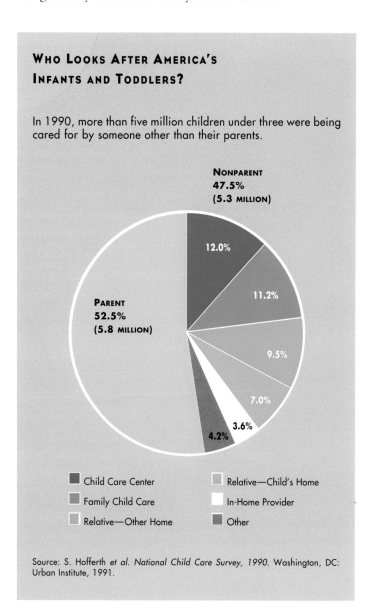

WHO LOOKS AFTER AMERICA'S INFANTS AND TODDLERS?

In 1990, more than five million children under three were being cared for by someone other than their parents.

NONPARENT
47.5%
(5.3 MILLION)

12.0%

11.2%

9.5%

7.0%

3.6%

4.2%

PARENT
52.5%
(5.8 MILLION)

■ Child Care Center   □ Relative—Child's Home
□ Family Child Care   □ In-Home Provider
□ Relative—Other Home   ■ Other

Source: S. Hofferth et al. National Child Care Survey, 1990. Washington, DC: Urban Institute, 1991.

society. Some employers now voluntarily offer parental leave, albeit usually unpaid. Many states require employers to provide basic parental leave benefits. In August 1993, the Family and Medical Leave Act (FMLA)—the nation's first family leave legislation—went into effect. This act requires employers of fifty or more people to provide to all eligible employees twelve weeks of unpaid, job-guaranteed leave with existing health benefits.

This is a laudable first step, but it does not address a number of problems. The task force recommends that the next step should be to include employers with fewer than fifty employees under the legislation; currently 50 to 60 percent of the workforce is excluded.

Recent research on the impact of parental leave policies indicates that small businesses are not adversely affected by state leave policies. Most businesses find it easy to comply with state laws, and small employers complying with state parental leave policies have incurred no greater costs than large employers.[5]

Broadening the act to cover more firms is only the first step. Unfortunately, a twelve-week leave, while helpful, does not ensure enough time for parents and the newborn child to develop the strong early relationships that are the foundation for healthy child development. The task force finds that leaves of four to six months would greatly benefit both infants and their parents.

Because the Family and Medical Leave Act and current employer leave policies do not include wage replacement, many parents must return to work much sooner than they wish. This is especially true for employed women from low-income households. These new mothers typically take less time off after childbirth than women from middle- and upper-income households, and almost one in five takes less than the medically advised minimum of six weeks. Only when some wage replacement is provided, do women from low-income families take leaves resembling those taken by middle- and upper-income women.[6]

All industrialized countries other than the United States, and many less developed nations, mandate both job-guaranteed parental leave and some provision for wage replacement. Possible policy options for financial support are:

- Expanded temporary disability insurance
- A modified unemployment compensation system
- A special benefit for parents with newborn or newly adopted children

Mechanisms for financing a paid national leave policy are not out of reach, if done on a phased-in basis. The responsibility for assuming these costs should be shared by employers, government, and employee contributions.

The Family and Medical Leave Act of 1993 establishes a Commission on Leave to assess the impact of the law and to recommend changes. The task force recommends that the Commission on Leave take a leadership role in evaluating implementation of the act and in studying policy options that would expand employee coverage, offer partial wage replacement, and

PAYING FOR PARENTAL LEAVE

The United States stands alone among major industrialized nations in not ensuring income protection for parental leave. This imposes particular hardship on working mothers, who must leave their infants within a few weeks after delivery. Most mothers who remain out of work after delivering a baby receive nothing from their employer or any other source. If they are lucky enough to be covered by temporary disability insurance (TDI)—as so few are—they will receive a check for full or partial wage replacement from employer-paid TDI for up to six months.

Now required by law for most employees in five states— California, Hawaii, New Jersey, New York, and Rhode Island— TDI could be expanded to cover the entire workforce. If so, it would provide partial wage replacement for some estimated 840,000 biological mothers.

As a means of providing paid parental leave, TDI offers several advantages:

- TDI can be structured as a national insurance system, administered by a federal agency or by state agencies within a federal regulatory framework.
- Funds can be generated from employee or employee contributions, or both, and collected through federal or state taxes.
- TDI can be financed on a pay-as-you-go basis, out of general revenues, or by means of insurance-type, risk-based premiums, as is done in the five states that now require TDI coverage.
- State and private insurance data can be used to calculate its costs.

Another approach would be modification of the unemployment compensation system. The current system benefits individuals who are fired or laid off; the program might be expanded to cover leaves of absence for families with a newborn infant. Austria and Canada have successfully introduced this plan. Austrian biological and adoptive parents who have qualifying employment histories receive paid leaves of 100 percent of weekly earnings up to the maximum insured wage; the government pays half, and employer and employee split the other half. In Canada, biological mothers and fathers who are covered by statutes and have qualifying employment histories receive 60 percent of wages up to the maximum insured wage during maternity and parenting leave; employers and employees pay the insurance premiums.

permit a longer leave. In addition, independent research should be conducted on the impact of policy options, including their costs and benefits, so that there is a knowledge base upon which to consider the next steps in family leave.

When surveyed, parents repeatedly state that they would like their employers to institute not only parental leave, but also a wide range of policies that support their role as parents. They want

- Gradual transition back to work
- Flexible time schedules and part-time work
- Financial assistance with sick child care
- Child care assistance through pretax deductions for child care, direct payments, on-site or nearby child care, more accessible facilities, or referral services[7]

Employers, especially those in the Fortune 1000 group, are increasingly finding it good business to respond to these needs. Smaller companies are more likely to respond to employees' work–family needs when they employ professionals than when they employ hourly-wage workers. Companies of all sizes are more likely to institute "work support"—services such as dependent care assistance plans or child care resource and referral that help employees work without distraction—than "family support" policies such as flexible time or parental leave that allow employees to be there for their children when needed.[8]

PARENTS NEED TIME TO GET TO KNOW THEIR INFANTS, TO UNDERSTAND THEIR BABIES' RHYTHMS, PATTERNS, AND PREFERENCES.

The task force recommends that all employers assist parents in ways that are consistent with the needs of both the workplace *and* the family. For example, employers should implement a range of policies such as flexible work schedules, job sharing, child care resource and referral assistance, and on-site or nearby child care.

ENSURE QUALITY CHILD CARE FOR INFANTS AND TODDLERS

For healthy development, infants and toddlers need close relationships with a small number of caring people, beginning with their parents and later including other adults. Infants and toddlers develop these relationships in safe, predictable, intimate settings—in their homes and child care settings. The importance of this process should be a core concern of parent education.

Quality child care programs for our youngest children share these characteristics:

- The environment is safe and comfortable.
- Children receive care in small groups.
- Each adult worker is responsible for only a few children.
- Personnel are well prepared and adequately paid.
- The program encourages parent involvement and is linked to comprehensive health and nutrition services.

Unfortunately, such environmental and staff characteristics are seen in only a small number of child care settings. To begin to address the crisis of substandard child care quality, the task force recommends action in three areas:

- Establish consistent standards of quality for infant and toddler child care.
- Require training for infant and toddler child care providers.
- Improve compensation for child care providers.

Establish Consistent Standards of Quality for Infant and Toddler Child Care

In looking for child care, most parents search for someone who will treat their child as special, as they themselves do.[9] Parents want their child to receive individualized attention from a sensitive and competent adult. They want a person who truly enjoys caring for young children, a person who will delight in singing, reading, talking, and playing with their baby. To parents, these qualities of individualized and loving care have little to do with formal standards. Most parents describe quality child care as "good parenting"; they believe that caregivers, not regulations, ensure high quality. Parents are skeptical of rules, and they support government involvement in limited doses, recognizing the utility of only the most basic health and safety standards. Even if they like more state monitoring in theory, they doubt its effectiveness in practice.

But child care professionals emphasize the enforcement of consistent standards as the key to high quality. A few consistent standards—appropriately monitored and enforced—can help achieve exactly what parents want. For example, a program that assigns a small number of children to each staff member goes far toward achieving individualized attention for every child. Similarly, standards for training can help ensure that adults interact appropriately with every child, because caring for multiple children from different families requires specialized preparation. Training makes a measurable difference: when providers have learned more about how children grow and develop, they are more likely to offer warmer and more sensitive care than providers with less

WHY QUALITY CHILD CARE MATTERS

Quality child care enables a young child to become emotionally secure, socially competent, and intellectually capable. The single most important factor in quality care is the relationship between the child and the caregiver. Children who receive warm and sensitive caregiving are more likely to trust caregivers, to enter school ready and eager to learn, and to get along well with other children.

The quality of caregiver–child relations depends in part on the sensitivity of the caregiver and in part on the ratio of caregivers to children, the number of children in a group, and the education and training levels of the caregiver. A quality program also attends to the basic issues of health and safety and emphasizes a partnership between parents and caregivers.

Children who receive inadequate or barely adequate care are more likely later to feel insecure with teachers, to distrust other children, and to face possible later rejection by other children. Rejection by other children appears to be a powerful predictor of unhappy results, including early dropping out of school and delinquency.

training.[10] When caregivers are sensitive and stay in the job long enough, children form bonds with them. These bonds do not in any way interfere with attachments to parents; instead, they supplement them.

Despite the evidence that standards establish the preconditions for quality child care, government policy lags behind. At present, child care regulation rests largely with state governments; more important, these standards are varied, weak, or even nonexistent. For instance, one state allows one adult to care for three infants and another allows one adult to care for twelve infants; twenty-three states do not set any standards for group size.[11] Virtually all states allow infants and toddlers to be cared for by providers who have not completed high school, have no training specific to infant and toddler development, and have received less than five hours of annual in-service training.[12]

The task force recommends that states review, upgrade, and implement consistent child care standards for quality child care. States must identify and agree to a few, fundamental standards and then establish an incentive plan with timetables for gradual adoption. Whether child care occurs in Massachusetts, Missippi, or Montana, child care standards must consistently promote quality throughout the United States. Such standards should apply to centers, family child care homes, and other birth-to-three programs such as Head Start Parent–Child Centers. Regardless of funding sources, the standards should address

- Child-to-staff ratios
- Group size
- Preparation and qualifications of staff
- Health and safety
- Linkage to other community services

In working toward better quality child care, many partners must support these baseline standards. Already, many cities and towns throughout our nation are attempting to devise workable mechanisms to ensure quality child care. In supporting consistent standards for group child care, it is not our intent to pose hardships for informal situations that are working well in communities and neighborhoods. Rather, we encourage communities to develop mechanisms to include these informal providers in local child care networks and to facilitate their compliance with the performance standards.

Professional groups must also play a critical role. Quality child care standards have already been proposed by many professional groups,

including the National Association for the Education of Young Children and the collaborative effort of the American Public Health Association and the American Academy of Pediatrics called "Caring for Our Children." States should draw on the work of these organizations.

The role of the federal government must also be strengthened to improve child care policy. In the past five years, Congress has established new initiatives through the Child Care and Development Block Grant (CCDBG) and the Family Support Act, as well as increasing funds for programs such as Head Start and for the care of children of military personnel. The federal government has permitted these programs to be implemented with a variety of standards and financing arrangements. With careful coordination between the Congress and the executive branch, the federal government can serve as a powerful force in linking child care funding, quality, and equity.

The task force recommends that all new and reauthorized federal funding for child care, including CCDBG, the At-Risk Child Care Program, and the Family Support Act Child Care Program, be modeled after the 1990 Head Start reauthorization. This reauthorization directed that 25 percent of new funds be spent on quality enhancements such as improved training, better facilities, and staff compensation. We urge that this money be coordinated at the state level and dedicated to promoting quality child care programs for infants and toddlers through investments in stronger standards, improved training, better facilities, and higher staff compensation. It is unacceptable to use public dollars to support a child care system that is serving our youngest children so poorly.

To protect society's investments, the federal government can also help states adopt and monitor state standards for child care.

- First, the federal government can provide financial incentives to states to adopt better standards, to establish timetables for the enactment of those standards, and to monitor progress toward enforcing them.

- Second, the federal government should collect and publish annual data about the average cost of care in various settings, the content of each state's child care standards, and the level of compliance with these standards. States should also be encouraged to support communities in providing useful resource and referral services to enhance parents' choices.

Require Training for Infant and Toddler Child Care Providers

In many cases, child care providers are the only adults other than parents who have daily contact with infants and toddlers. As such, they play a critical role in fostering the child's healthy development. Currently, many providers of child care lack specific preparation for their jobs: some have no training whatsoever, and others have received only a few hours of in-service training in child development. Moreover, few incentives exist to encourage further training. To ensure that child care settings nurture children, protect

their health and safety, and prepare them for later school success, better qualified staff are essential.[13]

Adults who are caring for children under three need to know about this unique period in a child's life. They need practical information about how infants and toddlers develop; how to cope with children's unique temperaments, rates of growth, and communication styles; how to foster healthy emotional and physical growth; and how to create respectful partnerships with children's families. Caregivers need training to maintain a safe and healthy environment and to identify physiological and developmental problems. Preparation should include both course work and service practicums. In this way, novice child care providers can be mentored by more highly trained, experienced infant-and-toddler specialists. Meaningful credentials should be granted upon completion of such training.

The task force recommends that specific training be a condition for providing group care for infants and toddlers. Current child care providers who lack such training should be given the opportunity to receive it on the job. For those already trained, a system of meaningful continuing education credits might also be established. This system would require that, over a set period, all providers take a certain number of courses; this type of system has advanced the professionalism of teachers, nurses, physicians, social workers, and psychologists over the past few decades.

NEW CAREERS FOR CHILD CARE PROFESSIONALS

Those who enter the child care field find few opportunities for training and career development:

- Funding for training is limited and sporadic. As a result, most caregivers have no access to training.
- Where training programs exist, incentives to participate are few or nonexistent. Beyond the entry level, few programs offer a sequence of training activities linked to career advancement steps.
- Most training situations fail to prepare caregivers to work with a wide range of children and families. They do not offer specialized training needed to care for children at particular developmental stages, or with particular life experiences.
- Caregivers in general cannot earn college credits by enrolling in a training program.

There are signs of progress, such as financial support for training under the federal Child Care and Development Block Grant program enacted in 1991. Federal and state policymakers are beginning to show interest in caregiver training, and planning to improve training has begun in several states.

Fortunately, examples of promising practices do exist:

- Since 1985, the California Child Care Initiative has been recruiting and training family child care providers. As of March 1993, it has generated 3,600 new licensed family child care homes, making 14,100 child care spaces available to children of all ages. More than 22,000 providers have received basic and advanced training at thirty-four sites across the state. The program offers incentives such as paying providers' membership fees to join professional associations, paying stipends for transportation to training, supplying vouchers for toys and equipment, and placing providers' names in local referral pools. The initiative has recently made more family child care materials available in Spanish and has developed a new recruitment initiative responding to the crisis in infant and toddler care.
- Families of children with disabilities who live in rural settings face particular difficulties in finding appropriate child care. In Montana, the Educational Home Model Outreach Program provides training and technical assistance to child care centers and family child care homes that care for children with and without disabilities. The program offers the particular skills needed to care for children with motor impairments. The project offers advice to other providers via a toll-free telephone line and a newsletter.
- In 1989, Delaware inaugurated the nation's first comprehensive statewide plan for career development in early care and education. The program has opened a resource center for child care providers in each of the state's three counties. It has involved the eight colleges in Delaware that offer early childhood curriculum in a pilot project that enables caregivers to earn college credits.

The task force recognizes that better training cannot resolve all the complex problems of child care. However, attention to training is a relatively inexpensive strategy for improving quality.[14] Further, it is a wise and cost-effective strategy to link all training initiatives to career development within the field. Individuals who obtain entry-level training should receive credit towards college associate and bachelor's degree programs. The task force also recommends that federal and state funds facilitate such training efforts. These funds should be used in several ways. First, they could help to create infant and toddler child care training systems throughout the country, ensuring that all states receive help and technical support. Funds could also help disseminate the best infant and toddler training materials for caregivers. The dissemination of training materials, along with the implementation of statewide training systems, would go a long way toward improving child care services to young children throughout the United States. However, the task force recognizes that attracting and retaining high-quality individuals to the child care field will always be constrained as long as salaries are so low.

Improve Compensation for Caregivers

Experienced child care providers who love their jobs leave them in high numbers because of low salaries and inadequate benefits. In a multisite study of center-based care, 70 percent of the staff left their jobs between 1988 and 1992. Between 1991 and 1992, staff turnover was 26 percent. This figure is close to three times the annual turnover reported by U.S. companies; it is nearly five times the 5.6 percent turnover rate reported for public school teachers.[15] With such high turnover rates, the quality of care deteriorates. Infants, toddlers, and their parents need to know they can count on the same well-prepared adults providing care over an extended period.

EXPERIENCED CHILD CARE PROVIDERS WHO LOVE THEIR JOBS LEAVE THEM IN HIGH NUMBERS BECAUSE OF LOW SALARIES AND INADEQUATE BENEFITS.

To sustain quality child care services, therefore, we must improve the compensation of child care providers. In 1990 the average annual salary for providers in centers was about $11,000. In regulated family child care homes, the average revenue received was $10,000 annually; half received less than $8,000 per year.[16] Nonregulated providers averaged $1,961 per year. Even providers with college training or degrees are woefully underpaid. Typically, child care professionals earn only half as much as equally prepared early childhood professionals working within the public school system.[17] Without pay increases, high levels of staff turnover will continue; training will serve only to prepare providers and teachers for their next (higher-paying) job, probably outside the early childhood field.

The goal should be to establish pay levels that are competitive across professions that call for equivalent educational qualifications and job responsibilities. Staff also need to receive benefits that include health insurance, sick leave, retirement, paid vacation, and workers' compensation.

But who will finance increased provider pay and benefits? At present, increased costs are passed on to the child's family, making it more difficult to find high-quality child care that is also affordable. This market-driven system has some serious faults that are burdensome to families. Pay raises to staff must not be solely contingent on a family's ability to pay fair wages. Just as with public education and health care, the costs of child care services must be valued as a public good that must be partially subsidized by government and industry. Individual families must not be "priced out" of quality child care.

The business and government sectors are beginning to turn their attention to child care quality, but a larger, more sustained commitment is necessary. Corporations can help by creating public–private partnerships to sponsor individual child care providers or centers that serve the communities from which they draw their labor force. Federal, state, and local governments all need to contribute to narrowing the differential between the costs of quality care and what is now affordable for many families. They can do so through incentives and innovative partnerships with nonprofit agencies and the private sector. These government and business initiatives should invest wisely in the people who are working in child care.

The task force recommends two strategies for improving provider compensation:

- First, tie higher salaries and better benefits to the completion of specialized training. Benefits supplement compensation and also enhance working conditions and job satisfaction.

- Second, provide incentive or salary enhancement grants to child care centers and family child care networks that provide quality care as defined by state standards or by professional organizations.

Staff should be rewarded when they complete specialized training and demonstrate classroom competence, perhaps through programs tied to higher pay or bonuses. Other ways of upgrading the status of child care work include conferring credentials or higher ranks in the child care profession. Training programs should also be targeted at those caregivers who need it, at a price they can afford and at a time that is convenient. For instance, North Carolina has developed the T.E.A.C.H. (Teacher Education and Compensation Helps) early childhood education project, which links training to compensation. The program reimburses child care providers for tuition, books, and travel; it also provides released time for providers in both centers and family child care homes. The provider is compensated while taking courses by receiving either a 4 to 5 percent raise or a comparable bonus. After completing the specially designed college course, the practitioner receives a 3 percent raise.

ARMY ACTION ON PAY BRINGS QUICK RESULTS

The U.S. Army provides child care for 90,000 children at some 250 facilities worldwide. In 1990 the Army undertook major reforms of its child care system. What it found when it examined the situation at Fort Stewart in Georgia was typical—and it was troubling. Child-to-staff ratios were high (6:1 for infants and 13:1 for three-year-olds). Even more disturbing was a staff turnover rate that significantly exceeded the national annual average of 40 percent: Brigadier General Raymond Roe characterized turnover as "horrible—constant. Some people estimated it at 300 percent." Turnover has consequences for infants and toddlers: "What we call turnover," Deborah Phillips, an expert in child development, said, "they experience as loss."

The Army found that the main reason for turnover was pay. The average pay for child care workers at Fort Stewart was $4.47 per hour, less than the national average, and with no benefits. "We pay higher salaries in our society to people who take care of dogs in kennels and cars in parking lots than to the adults who take care of our children in child care," according to Phillips. Seeking to increase staff pay while keeping care affordable for parents, Fort Stewart commanders, under the authority of the Military Child Care Act of 1990, raised staff pay from $4.47 to $6.41 per hour, the same as other entry-level jobs on the post. Turnover dropped dramatically.

Fort Stewart then implemented a mandatory staff training program and career ladder. Caregivers learn about child development and how to plan activities that engage the children. "We were more like babysitters at one time," a staff member observed. "Now we get to be professionals, we get to be teachers." The Army also improved the teacher:child ratios, which now meet the standards developed by the National Association for the Education of Young Children. Infants are constantly held, played with, or talked to, rather than consigned to swings or cribs.

These reforms doubled the cost to $100 per week per child. Parents pay half, and the Army subsidizes the balance. Army commanders believe that quality child care pays off: it enhances retention of soldier–parents, relieves stress, and improves force readiness. "If I'm deployed, if I go to the field, I just don't have to worry," one soldier said of her daughter. "I know she's going to be well taken care of."

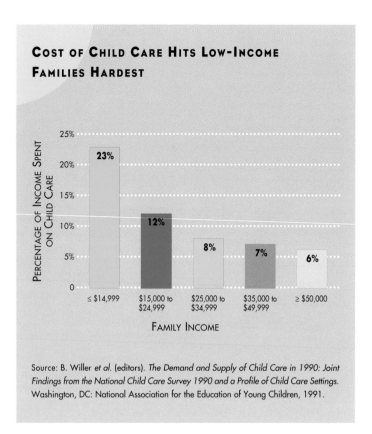

COST OF CHILD CARE HITS LOW-INCOME FAMILIES HARDEST

PERCENTAGE OF INCOME SPENT ON CHILD CARE

25%
20%
15%
10%
5%
0

23%
12%
8%
7%
6%

≤ $14,999 | $15,000 to $24,999 | $25,000 to $34,999 | $35,000 to $49,999 | ≥ $50,000

FAMILY INCOME

Source: B. Willer *et al.* (editors). *The Demand and Supply of Child Care in 1990: Joint Findings from the National Child Care Survey 1990 and a Profile of Child Care Settings.* Washington, DC: National Association for the Education of Young Children, 1991.

PROVIDE PARENTS WITH AFFORDABLE CHILD CARE OPTIONS

Traditionally, our nation has asked parents to invest substantial resources in the care and education of young children, especially in the years before children enter the public school system. Because no cash transactions take place, these childrearing services have not been included in our nation's official Gross Domestic Product (GDP). Nonetheless, the value of this "non-monetized" economic activity is large—in fact, it affects many of the "goods and services" that matter most in the lives of young children and their parents.[18]

The Committee on Economic Development has recently estimated that the "total value of unpaid housework is approximately one third of the conventionally measured GDP. Specifically, the value of the services and goods devoted to the care and education of children is approximately two to four percent of the GDP, or on the order of $120 billion–$240 billion annually."[19] In recent years, as mothers more often work, parents have increasingly paid—in actual dollars—for non-parental child care services. This country is just beginning to realize just how expensive quality child care actually is.

When they realize how much child care costs, most parents are astonished. Costs for one child range from $40 to $200 per week.[20] Over the course of a year, families on average pay $2,565 for family child care or $3,173 for center-based child care.[21] As might be expected, infant and toddler care that is high in quality costs more, from $185 to $200 per week in some communities.[22] Some families would thus have to pay $8,000 to $10,000 each year for child care.

All families want to give their children the best care possible, but these outlays are much too high for most. Overall, the less families earn, the higher the proportion of their income that is spent for child care. Families earning less than $15,000 annually often spend a quarter of their income for child care—this is as much as many families spend on housing. Single mothers spend twice as much of their income on child care as two-parent families do.[23]

Even given these costs, most parents know that they have little choice in today's economy but to work.[24] Employed mothers, whose salaries are generally modest, need care that is inexpensive enough to make working worthwhile.[25] At the same time, mothers do not want their young children to suffer because they have to work.

Child care providers, too, feel torn. Many providers would love to hire a more highly trained staff and to pay them higher salaries.

TAPPING NEW RESOURCES FOR QUALITY CHILD CARE

New partners are beginning to take the lead in helping parents to find quality, affordable child care. These new initiatives may foretell dramatic shifts in the way America's vital institutions accommodate family and workplace responsibilities in the future. The following initiatives represent important new ways of promoting quality child care.

- **Corporations** can provide for their own employees and become models for approaches that the business community can take in creating more family-friendly working conditions. For example, in 1988, the Dayton Hudson Corporation began "Family-to-Family" as a collaboration with local nonprofit child care resource and referral agencies to train and accredit family child care providers. By 1992, Dayton Hudson recognized the value of a nationwide public awareness and consumer education campaign on quality child care, and launched "Child Care Aware" in collaboration with leading child care organizations. Child Care Aware encourages parents to consider quality issues in selecting child care services through innovative marketing techniques such as shopping bags that explain the value of quality child care. It helps them locate such services with advice from local resource and referral agencies, helps develop strong parent–caregiver partnerships, builds recognition of child care as a profession, and educates the public about the importance of quality child care for society.

- **State** governments can support innovative financing arrangements to provide capital to child care providers. For example, the State of Illinois has entered into an arrangement to issue tax-exempt bonds, repayable in ten years, with a philanthropic guarantee as collateral. The resulting Illinois Facilities Fund will provide capital to develop ten centers run by child care providers, who will lease the facilities for ten years and will assume ownership when the bond issue is paid off. The financing is expected to strengthen and improve child care centers in disadvantaged neighborhoods. The ten large centers will be fully equipped and curriculum-based and will have support for staff development and training; they should serve as laboratories for further understanding of the economic growth of child care and the needs of families.

- **Banks** can add child care programs to their activities under the Community Reinvestment Act (CRA). The act requires federally insured mortgage-lending institutions to make funds available for community and neighborhood reinvestment at affordable interest rates. If banks identify child care as a "community need" under the CRA, they can make loans to providers as part of their obligations to assist low- and moderate-income neighborhoods. Affordable capital is chronically short in many such neighborhoods.

- **Philanthropic** and nonprofit organizations, including private and community foundations, can take the lead in identifying child care as a critical community issue. They can bring together representatives of employers and employees, persuade local governments and grantmakers to take an interest, and underwrite pilot programs. In 1987, for example, United Way of Massachusetts Bay formed the Child Care Initiative with other foundations and corporations to capitalize a loan fund. The loan fund is intended, in the short term, to provide capital to child care providers for expansion and stabilization of their operations, to ensure investment in centers serving low-income children, and to encourage more businesslike management practices among nonprofit providers. In the longer term, the fund is expected to draw attention to the facilities and capital needs of child care providers, who are often undercapitalized.

But providers are also reluctant to raise fees for care. After all, if parents already complain about paying $3,000 or $4,000 a year, how can one ask for another $1,000? Instead, providers try hard to keep costs down. They hold fees down by keeping staff wages low or even reducing them, by hiring fewer staff, eliminating benefits, and cutting corners on quality.

A promising strategy for making quality child care more available is to develop more differentiated staffing patterns. Such patterns would combine an increased number of entry-level providers with more highly trained caregivers. Initiatives are being developed to help low-income adults, welfare recipients, older volunteers, and students interested in national service to receive training and entry-level employment in child care. For example, with little additional public expenditure, mothers with infants and young children could be offered an opportunity to pursue education in basic health care, child development, nutrition, and other skills needed to care for their own children as well as the children of others. Mothers who satisfactorily complete the first level of training could be certified as qualified entry-level infant care providers in either family- or center-based child care settings. After additional training, these women could become certified as child care providers. Such an initiative could significantly increase the supply of competent caregivers while at the same time reducing the public and private costs of inadequate care. Another route to a child

OVERWHELMINGLY, TODAY'S PARENTS WOULD LIKE TO SEE BOTH GOVERNMENT AND BUSINESS ASSIST ALL FAMILIES BY ENSURING ACCESS TO AN ADEQUATE SUPPLY OF AFFORDABLE CHILD CARE.

care career may be through the recently enacted national service program. Students seeking a stipend and loan forgiveness through this program may provide a relatively inexpensive and highly motivated source of assistance in adequately staffing many overburdened child care settings.

Overwhelmingly, today's parents would like to see both government and business assist all families by ensuring access to an adequate supply of affordable child care.[26] Parents want businesses to offer benefit plans that include onsite or nearby child care and flexible work schedules.[27]

The federal government already offers some assistance with child care to families at all income levels. Depending on actual family income, this support comes in the form of a tax credit, voucher, or direct subsidies to providers. Middle- and upper-income families receive assistance largely through the Dependent Care Tax Credit (DCTC); lower-income and poor families receive subsidies through CCDBG, the Family Support Act, and Head Start. But these measures are not sufficient.

The task force recognizes that making quality child care affordable for parents is a complex problem for this country. The federal government is struggling with a large deficit and tight spending rules, and states have already stretched their finances to assume more responsibility for child care. At the same time, resources directed to the support of child care are inadequate. In this economic climate, the task force recommends that preference be given to providing more financial support to poor and moderate-income families so that they can choose quality child care. We propose two strategies.

First, the federal government should channel substantial new money into child care in order to make it more affordable for parents. This money should go to child care providers, permitting them to expand facilities and adopt sliding fee schedules. The new money could be provided in the form of supplementary block grants to the states for child care, though this is not the only possible channel. This new money should be designated to provide quality child care for children under three. Recognizing the fiscal stringency we face as a nation, we cannot recommend an infusion of new federal funds in the amounts sufficient to meet all or even most of the existing needs. Nevertheless, we believe it is urgent to make a "down payment" of enough federal money to expand and upgrade the child care facilities now available to the nation's youngest children. Regardless of whether increased funds are provided through welfare-related child care programs, Head Start, or other federal or state child care programs, all federal child care assistance must ensure the full and healthy development of infants and toddlers.

Second, the federal government should make the Dependent Care Tax Credit refundable in order to provide greater financial benefits to low-income families. Currently, the DCTC is used by families of all income levels. However, since it is non-refundable, poor and low-income families benefit least (and sometimes not at all) and upper-income families benefit most. Only 3 percent of the total credit goes to families in the bottom 30 percent of the income distribution, while 75 percent goes to families in the top half of the income distribution.[28]

JUST AS WITH PUBLIC EDUCATION AND HEALTH CARE, THE COSTS OF CHILD CARE SERVICES MUST BE VALUED AS A PUBLIC GOOD.

The additional costs of refundability could be made up by lowering the income levels at which the DCTC phases out or by decreasing the benefit levels for high-income families.[29] The task force recognizes that many moderate-income families need and take advantage of the DCTC. Because of this, we recommend careful study of the redistribution of the DCTC so that those low- and moderate-income families who need help in purchasing quality child care are not put at a greater financial disadvantage. In addition, the DCTC might be made payable at regular intervals, so that parents would be more likely to use it to purchase quality child care. As things stand, most parents are unlikely to connect the DCTC benefit with their direct child care expenditures. After paying for child care on a weekly or monthly basis, parents receive this benefit only once a year, when they file their previous year's taxes on April 15th.

DEVELOP NETWORKS OF FAMILY-CENTERED CHILD CARE PROGRAMS FOR INFANTS AND TODDLERS

Virtually every American community has produced a patchwork of child care, including licensed centers, regulated family child care, unregulated family child care, and informal care by relatives. Most parents become aware of their many choices only with their first child, when issues of how and where to find child care first become important to them.

Yet all too often, the seams that hold this child care quilt together are frayed. In most communities, providers function in almost total isolation—they have little opportunity to

share ideas, learn new skills, or provide support and guidance to one another. This isolation is particularly apparent in family child care and care by relatives—the types of care most popular for infants and toddlers.

The many patches of American child care can and must be stitched together. Local child care networks have proven effective, offering numerous benefits:

- Networks alleviate the isolation experienced by many child care providers, particularly those who take care of infants and toddlers in their homes.[30]

- They provide facilities, resources, and materials for professional development activities and enrichment for groups of children.

- They offer parents a well-known, accessible, unbiased source of information and advice as they sort through various child care options. This is especially important for parents who may be new to a community (or to this country), who do not speak English, or who have low incomes.

- They link child care providers with a wide variety of related health, educational, and social services.

The network concept is already working successfully in France. Family day care networks (crèches familiales) link from six to as many as thirty-five homes. Each network is directed by a specially trained pediatric nurse who coordinates administration, training, activities, and equipment lending. The nurse–director hires child care providers, supervises their training by qualified staff, matches each provider with two or three children, maintains contact with municipal officials, and even organizes backup services for children whose providers get sick. The network staff organizes small group sessions for caregivers and children. During these sessions, caregivers can receive training, information, or social support while children participate in educational activities.

Similar efforts are also under way in the United States. For instance, some areas of Los Angeles have a network system that connects center and family child care. Child care centers serve as the hub and resource for neighborhood family child care homes. Parents are able to contact family child care providers through the center. This structure has given not only assistance, but also credibility, to the family child care providers and the parents they serve.

The task force recommends that every community develop a child care network linking all child care programs and offering consumers a variety of child care settings, including homes, centers, and Head Start programs. Communities could secure funds for these networks through a combination of public and private sources.

Communities should especially encourage participation in these networks by relative and family child care providers. Many infants and toddlers are cared for by relatives or in small family care homes. The smaller setting and more personal care are particularly appropriate for such young children, but the caregivers vary widely in education and experience. By participating in a family child care network, these providers could alleviate their isolation and improve their skills. Educational resources such as toys and books could also be made available. Through the workings of such networks, children in these settings might benefit from a significantly improved child care experience.[31]

In order to work most efficiently, a child care network should have three key features:
- It must be locally developed and operated, coordinating services within a neighborhood or town with a minimum of red tape.
- It must be comprehensive, including all existing child care services, such as public and private nonprofit and for-profit child care centers, as well as family and relative child care. It should also enable children with disabilities to participate fully.
- It must have as its center an institution that is central to its particular community—for example, a child care center, a Head Start program serving infants and toddlers, a local elementary school, or the neighborhood family and child center.

Clearly, to be effective, the network must draw on the energy of the community, involving people who know best what its parents and children need.

IN MOST COMMUNITIES, PROVIDERS FUNCTION IN ALMOST TOTAL ISOLATION— THEY HAVE LITTLE OPPORTUNITY TO SHARE IDEAS, LEARN NEW SKILLS, OR PROVIDE SUPPORT AND GUIDANCE TO ONE ANOTHER.

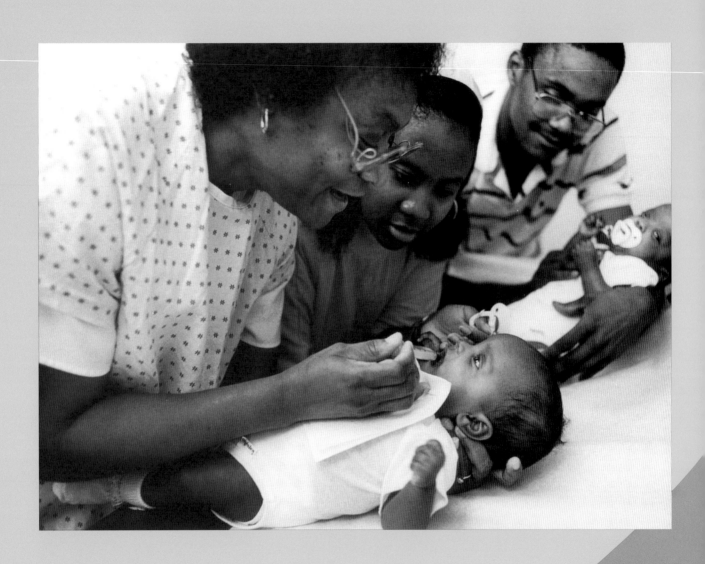

ENSURE GOOD HEALTH
AND PROTECTION

Few social programs offer greater long-term benefits for American society than guaranteeing good health care for all infants and toddlers. We realize the return on that investment when fewer children suffer from preventable illnesses and disabilities and when fewer parents bear the burden of caring for sick children and paying their medical bills. We realize the return when more healthy children and adolescents succeed in school, form a more productive workforce, and in time become better parents. We don't have to guess about the benefits of early health care; indeed, in no other area of social policy can costs and benefits be calculated so precisely. For example, every dollar spent on childhood immunizations saves ten dollars in later medical costs.[1]

Good health, of course, involves more than medical care. Being healthy also means being safe. At present, many infants and toddlers are not safe. Some grow up in neighborhoods where a walk to the grocery store or an afternoon in the playground may be fraught with danger. Some spend long stretches, while their parents work, in substandard child care, under the supervision of underpaid, distracted babysitters, or in the care of brothers or sisters who themselves need more adult attention. And too many are at risk even when cared for by their own parents: some may suffer neglect or outright abuse; others may have parents who do not realize that their practices, or the setting they've provided, are unsafe. They may lack the information they need to ensure adequate nutrition, secure essential health services, or block a toddler's access to toxic household products. These children are at increased risk for health problems or injuries that in most cases need not occur.

Yet, here too, public policy takes little account of ensuring the health and protection of children under three. Similarly, employers and their health insurance carriers focus little attention on preventive health care, which is particularly important for young children. Communities take little responsibility for creating environments in which families with infants and toddlers are safe and protected.

THE SCOPE OF HEALTH CARE FOR VERY YOUNG CHILDREN

All very young children need good health and medical care if they are to develop optimally. Even healthy infants need a full spectrum of health care services. This care must begin *before* birth, with comprehensive prenatal care for the mother, and must continue after birth, with regular and specialized care that is both preventive and curative. In all cases, services must be appropriate to the child's age and must include developmental assessments. Comprehensive care also provides parents with counseling about health care issues and helps them gain access to social and medical services. If properly provided, this array of services can ensure appropriate health care for all infants and toddlers.

GOOD HEALTH INVOLVES MORE THAN MEDICAL CARE. BEING HEALTHY ALSO MEANS BEING SAFE.

Unfortunately, not all young children now receive adequate health care. The American Academy of Pediatrics recommends nine well-child visits by age two, but fewer than 50 percent of all two-year-olds have visited the pediatrician that often. Children in low-income, minority families receive even less attention. Most of these children receive care only in hospital emergency rooms and only when acute illness or serious injury strikes.[2]

Well-child visits and timely acute care visits lead to early detection and correction of conditions that, if untreated, might impair young children's physical, intellectual, and social development.[3] For example, screening for lead level and follow-up treatment of a toddler who lives in a turn-of-the-century house can minimize the possibility of mental retardation due to lead ingestion. A child whose middle ear infection is diagnosed and treated early will probably not sustain a hearing loss.

"Immunization provides the starkest example of the power of prevention to save or prolong lives, prevent significant disability, and lower medical costs," according to the Office of Technology Assessment,[4] and the American Academy of Pediatrics recommends that all two-year-olds be immunized against several common childhood diseases. Yet immunization remains haphazard, with predictable consequences. Between 1981 and 1988 approximately 3,000 cases of measles were reported each year. As immunization rates decreased in the late 1980s, the number of cases skyrocketed, reaching 26,000 in 1990.[5] By 1992, immunization rates for two-year-olds were 30 percent in a few states and were below 60 percent in most. Then, as immunization rates picked up again in 1993, the incidence of measles began to drop.[6]

Children in Poverty Are at Risk for Poor Health

The supply of health professionals and the quality of child health care vary significantly by community: the most inadequate prenatal and child health services are found in low-income, minority, and transient communities. As a result, our poorest communities are plagued by high rates of infant mortality, low-birthweight babies, communicable childhood diseases, and child abuse.[7] Many of the tragedies represented by these statistics are preventable.

IMMUNIZATION: THE GOAL
FOR ALL TWO-YEAR-OLDS

Communicable diseases have become more common among this nation's children. The reason for this is clear: far too few two-year-olds are being adequately immunized in the United States. Many Americans find this distressing, considering the relatively low cost of immunizations and the huge benefits: Every dollar spent on immunization saves ten dollars in later medical costs. Two initiatives are mounting campaigns to ensure that all children are immunized by age two.

EVERY CHILD BY TWO

In 1991 former First Lady Rosalyn Carter and Betty Bumpers, wife of Senator Dale Bumpers of Arkansas, joined forces to ensure that babies receive their immunizations on time. Their Every Child by Two campaign is helping to get the word out to parents on the importance of early immunization, it is encouraging states and local health departments to increase access to immunization services, and it is promoting long-term policy changes that will ensure full immunization for all children by age two.

The organization has enlisted the cooperation of the spouses of governors and members of Congress, as well as involving elected officials and representatives of more than fifty national organizations, health providers, and concerned community leaders. Campaigns have been conducted in twenty-six states, and technical assistance and resources are being provided to state and community immunization projects.

SAN ANTONIO'S IMMUNIZATION PROJECT

To make certain that children are fully immunized, local communities must reach out to parents, communicate the importance of immunizing young children, and then make it easy for parents to comply. San Antonio is one city that is leading the way.

The city's computerized health data system is the backbone of the initiative. The system records all births and is linked to all hospital emergency rooms, public health clinics, and health care providers, allowing neighborhoods with low immunization rates to be identified and targeted for special outreach efforts. In addition, when a child develops a disease that can be prevented with a vaccine, other children living in the same neighborhood can be identified and immunized if necessary.

The immunization message is communicated in both English and Spanish through radio and television public service announcements, billboards, and bench ads at bus stops. Trained staff members also go door-to-door to bring parents information and encourage them to act. In addition, staff members at WIC nutrition services clinics assess children's immunization status and give vaccines as needed. Within two years, immunization rates among children receiving WIC improved from 40 to 83 percent.

Low-income families want to make the best possible decisions about their infant's or toddler's health, but their options are often limited. Many parents lack the money to buy health care services or pay health insurance premiums. They may be unable to rent a home in a safe neighborhood. And they may not be able to afford healthy, nutritious food.

Malnutrition during the first two years of life has much more devastating consequences than at any other time, inhibiting normal growth and development. Children growing up in poverty suffer from higher rates of malnutrition and anemia than other children. In one urban hospital, low-income two-year-olds were 40 percent more likely than other toddlers to be severely underweight and clinically malnourished. They were 60 percent more

A SUPPLEMENTAL FOOD PROGRAM: BUILDING ON SUCCESS

WIC, the Special Supplemental Food Program for Women, Infants, and Children, was established in the early 1970s. It provides highly nutritious food to low-income women who are pregnant or breastfeeding and to their children up to the age of five. WIC also provides the women with information and education on nutrition. The program links the distribution of food to other health services, including prenatal care. According to the National Commission on Children's 1991 report *Beyond Rhetoric*, participation in WIC reduces by 15 to 25 percent the chance that a high-risk pregnant woman will deliver a premature or low-birthweight baby. It increases the likelihood that these women will receive early, regular prenatal care and that their children will get regular pediatric care and immunizations. Mothers and children who are at greatest risk—those who are poor, minority, and poorly educated—benefit most.

WIC's cost-effectiveness has been clearly demonstrated. Because it significantly reduces the chances of prematurity and low birthweight and thus avoids extraordinary costs of neonatal intensive care that these conditions typically entail, the savings can be substantial. The average cost of providing WIC services to a woman throughout her pregnancy is estimated to be less than $250; the costs of sustaining a low-birthweight baby in a neonatal intensive care unit for one day are many times that amount. Despite its demonstrated success, however, WIC has never been fully funded. It currently serves some 4 million women and children, out of an eligible population of 7 million.

likely to suffer malnutrition in the winter months, when, researchers speculated, families diverted their limited funds from food to fuel.[8]

This finding suggests that malnutrition is most severe when poor and low-income parents have to choose among life's barest necessities. Even when federal nutrition assistance is available, it does not reach many poor children. Despite its proven effectiveness, the Women, Infants, and Children (WIC) program, which provides nutritional supplementation, reaches little more than half of all eligible families.[9]

When they do not have to choose between housing and food, low-income families attend to their children's nutritional needs. For example, iron deficiency is less common among children whose parents receive housing subsidies than among those whose parents do not. Housing subsidies cut rents in half for many recipients of Aid to Families with Dependent Children, thus freeing up money to spend on food.[10] Full funding of these subsidy programs might prove beneficial in reducing malnutrition among young children.

In poor neighborhoods, families with infants and toddlers are more likely to live in homes with hazards than are their more affluent counterparts. Poor children who live in old apartments or homes have high rates of accidental injury. They are also often exposed to toxic levels of lead that adversely affects brain development and functioning. Toxic lead levels appear to increase a child's risk of having a reading disability sixfold and of later dropping out of school sevenfold.[11] Additionally, many cases of childhood asthma are attributable to allergic responses to such household vermin as cockroaches, mites, and rodents. Rates of accidental injury are also higher in poor neighborhoods.

Millions of Children Receive Inadequate Health Care

Children in poverty are not alone in receiving inadequate health care. Many children receive substandard health care largely because of the lack of medical and health insurance. In 1992, 8.4 million children lacked access to health care services because they had no insurance, and millions more were insured for only part of the year.[12] Most children rely on working parents for health care coverage, yet nearly 80 percent of uninsured children are dependents of working parents.[13] Children lack insurance coverage for several reasons[14]:

- Increasing numbers of children now live with single mothers who work in low-paying service jobs without medical insurance.
- Employer health care benefits have declined over the past decade.
- If family coverage is offered, the employee often declines it because of the high cost of the premiums.

The current system of employer-based medical insurance thus leaves large gaps in health care benefits for children. Such gaps illustrate why the United States lags behind other nations in providing health care services to children. Except for South Africa, the United States is alone among industrialized nations in failing to provide health insurance for children.[15] This is short-sighted public policy; healthy children are more likely to grow into healthy, productive adults. Children covered by health insurance use health care services more often and have better health outcomes.[16] But nearly 13 percent of America's children do not have access to the health care services they need to grow up healthy.[17]

To move toward ensuring that infants and toddlers grow up healthy and protected, the task force recommends changes in public policy to

- Provide needed health care services for all infants and toddlers
- Protect infants and toddlers from injury and promote their health
- Create safe environments for infants and toddlers

EXCEPT FOR SOUTH AFRICA, THE UNITED STATES IS ALONE AMONG INDUSTRIALIZED NATIONS IN FAILING TO PROVIDE HEALTH INSURANCE FOR CHILDREN.

PROVIDE NEEDED HEALTH CARE SERVICES FOR ALL INFANTS AND TODDLERS

Health care reform has risen to the top of our national agenda. The prohibitive costs and limited access of our current health care system have sparked wide interest in reform. Many different measures are being introduced in Congress, and states are also struggling with health care reform. Complex issues and competing interests, including the urgent need to make health care reform work for children, will shape the outcomes.

Young children need comprehensive health care because their needs differ markedly from those of older children and adults. Infants' and toddlers' unique needs arise from their developmental vulnerability and the degree to which they are dependent on others—on their parents and on social and governmental institutions—for their health care.[18] To ensure that these needs are met, the task force concluded that policymakers should use a clinical standard of pediatric care to determine the amount, scope, and duration of child health care services and should include not only prenatal health services but also services for nonpregnant women that can affect future pregnancy, fetal development, and maternal health.

In 1979, the Select Panel for the Promotion of Child Health—a federal group composed of fifteen of the nation's leading health care professionals—began the most thorough review of this subject ever undertaken in this country. Fifteen years later, the task force agrees with the panel's conclusions[19]:

- Health care services for all children must be comprehensive, preventive, and primary, including well-child and acute-care visits, immunizations, newborn and periodic

health screening (such as PKU and lead exposure), preventive dental care, vision and hearing tests, and developmental and behavioral assessments.

- The 10 percent of children who have chronic or disabling conditions need, in addition, specially designed services and support.
- Comprehensive services include parental education and counseling.
- Access to health care must be ensured through services such as transportation to health facilities and translators who can speak with parents and children in their own language.

The task force identified two elements that would go farthest toward ensuring that children under three receive needed health care services. First, pregnant women, infants, and toddlers must be explicitly included in health care reform. Second, home visiting services should be available as part of comprehensive health services.

Include Children under Three in Health Care Reform

The task force supports the principle that health care reform should result in comprehensive health care services for all our nation's children. Universal primary and preventive care is the cornerstone of children's health services and is long overdue. (See the Appendix to this chapter, page 80, for a complete list of recommended services.) The task force agrees that the health care needs of infants and toddlers call for services that are broader in scope than those designed for older children and adults, and in certain instances they must be of greater intensity and duration than would be possible under a more general standard.

Some experts have suggested that within health care reform there needs to be a separate standard of coverage and service for children. This concept should be given serious consideration, as it would

- Guarantee that children's health care services take into account developmental and dependency needs
- Serve as an important organizing principle for systemic health reform and define necessary health care services for children[20]

Whatever health care coverage is adopted, many details will need to be resolved regarding the amount, duration and scope of benefits, and the adjustment of benefits within certain limits to meet the needs of different individuals and groups. It will also be necessary to balance cost containment with quality child health services.

Controlling costs can pose grave risks to quality. The connection is often glossed over in policy discussions, perhaps to make cost control seem less painful than it is. But cost control can result in poor-quality care or in less care—even for children, who are scarcely over-consumers of health care now. For example, many health plans now limit mothers and newborns to twenty-four hours of hospitalization following a normal delivery. Mothers for whom early discharge is a reasonable option are not distinguished from those for whom early discharge poses both medical and social risks. These plans even send a baby home without his or her mother if, after twenty-four hours, the mother is ill and the baby is fine.

In the absence of conscientious home monitoring of new mothers and babies, very early discharge runs directly counter to good pre-ventive medicine. Indeed, good practice calls for careful medical monitoring of both mother and infant for at least three days postpartum, as well as education and support for the new mother during that period. The less experienced or more socially high-risk the mother, the greater the need for this postpartum assistance. Yet short-term cost control is winning the day, and postpartum hospital stays grow ever shorter, even in the absence of other systems to provide the needed care and education.

COST CONTROL MUST BE ACCOMPANIED BY ADEQUATE PROVISIONS TO ENSURE HEALTH CARE QUALITY.

Cost control must be accompanied by adequate provisions to ensure health care quality. The design or revision of a benefits package must take into account not only budgetary considerations and national priorities, but also scientific criteria for adequate health and medical care. Meaningful grievance procedures must enable consumers and providers to protest unfair practices or unintended consequences. To achieve this, consumers and clinicians must work with policymakers in defining what constitutes a child health care service.

Clearly, money is the main barrier between America's young children and the health services they require; but other *non*financial barriers must also be surmounted.[21] These include

- *Capacity shortages*. Too few "appointment slots" are currently available to meet demand. Many communities do not have enough providers, especially pediatricians, family practitioners, and nurse practitioners.

- *Unfriendly services.* Unfriendly, hard-to-access services are an obstacle to care whose significance has not been fully appreciated. Even those parents who are motivated to seek out health services may be alienated when the clinic telephone is constantly busy or when they are put on hold for long blocks of time; when intake clerks are unresponsive; when staff spend more time determining how services will be paid for than gathering information about the health problem that brought the child there; when parents are given five minutes of a doctor's time after spending hours with their children in a waiting room; when paperwork is impossibly complicated; when interpreters are unavailable.

- *Undervaluing of preventive services.* Many parents who obtain health care when their children are sick are unlikely to use preventive services like well-child visits or immunizations, particularly when these services are not easily available. To seek out preventive services, parents must be motivated to ward off a future, hypothetical danger—not a current, real one. Moreover, mothers with fewer resources and less education, and many who are immigrants, may not immediately grasp the nature or importance of preventive services. Most important, prevention cannot be a high priority for those whose immediate concerns are adequate food, housing, and employment.

- *Lack of continuity.* Many young children do not receive the ongoing health care services they need because they do not have a primary health care provider. The collapse of the public health infrastructure in recent years has cut off many young children from the services they need.

Other barriers include the violence, drugs, and social isolation found in some impoverished inner-city neighborhoods—conditions associated with low levels of health care. Expectant mothers in these neighborhoods are far less likely to receive adequate prenatal care than those in more affluent locales; and preschool immunization rates are also low in these areas. Already over-stressed, these children and their families should not have to add inadequate health care to their list of everyday life problems.

Americans today do not have equal access to health care, and will not even with universal health insurance. Particularly for high-risk, low-income children and their families, health insurance does not automatically translate into health care; coverage is worthless if no primary care provider is available. The nation will have to do more than expand access to coverage.

The task force recommends that all pregnant women and all children receive comprehensive health care services that promote their health and well-being. We recommend that pregnant women and all children under three be the first to be included in a universal system. This is a "down payment"—assuring that children get a healthy start and have the greatest opportunity for a life of productivity and vigor.

Provide Home Visiting Services to Pregnant Women and Families with Infants and Toddlers

For more than a century, home visiting has existed in the United States as a strategy for delivering health care, information, and support services to pregnant women and families with young children. Today, home visiting ser-

vices are drawing attention as a promising preventive strategy. The General Accounting Office, numerous experts, and many commission reports have suggested that home visiting can help all newborns have a good start in life, can foster child development and school readiness, can encourage parents to take advantage of preventive health services, and can decrease the incidence of infant mortality, low birthweight, and child abuse.[22]

Because of these advantages, home visiting programs have increased in popularity. Many states now offer voluntary home visiting services to all new parents and provide more intensive services to at-risk families with young children. The task force recommends that home visiting services be offered on a volun-

tary basis as part of comprehensive health services to all first-time parents and their newborns. In addition, more intensive home visiting services should be available for certain at-risk groups of families that request them.

The task force concluded that the current practice of early hospital discharge after the birth of the newborn makes home visiting an attractive strategy during the first six weeks of a newborn's life. By providing at least one visit within the first two weeks, the home visitor can offer advice about infant feeding and support for breastfeeding; answer questions about newborn care; assess the newborn's general health; and provide information about preventive health care, family support services, and child care. The home visitor becomes an important link between the family and community services and supports.

HEALTHY FAMILIES AMERICA

In 1992, more than 2.9 million cases of suspected child abuse were reported, many of them among children from birth to three years of age. Research indicates that the best way to promote healthy child development, to strengthen families, and to prevent child abuse is to provide parents with education and support beginning with the birth of their first baby, ideally by means of a voluntary program of home visits.

Hawaii's Healthy Start Program is an effective model. This initiative provides an initial home visit and assessment of all families with newborns. "At-risk" families are identified and provided with family support, family crisis resolution strategies, and mental health services. Based on Healthy Start, Healthy Families America was launched in 1992 to lay the foundation for a nationwide neonatal home visiting program. Initiated by the National Committee to Prevent Child Abuse, in partnership with the Ronald McDonald Children's Charities, Healthy Families proposes to establish intensive home visitor programs in areas where parents lack education and support programs and to build onto existing programs wherever possible.

The need for such programs is particularly great where children are at greatest risk for abuse or neglect (that is, in communities with high percentages of low-birthweight babies, births to unmarried adolescents, and children living in poverty).

Community-based parent education and support programs exist in the United States, but few are statewide, comprehensive, and well-coordinated with other federal, state, and local programs. Healthy Families America intends to improve this situation. Efforts are under way in all fifty states to build a Healthy Families America system, and eleven states are operating small pilot programs.

The task force also determined that any effort to offer good health care to all infants and toddlers must reach young children whose parents live in impoverished, violent neighborhoods. It is precisely with these vulnerable children and mothers that the investment can have the highest payoff. Especially effective are comprehensive prenatal and infant services, in which trained nurses or paraprofessionals visit unmarried, adolescent, uneducated, or low-income mothers and their children. These programs have successfully encouraged expectant mothers to stop smoking, eat a balanced diet, use the WIC nutrition supplementation program, and seek childbirth education. In families that have been visited, the incidence of low-birthweight babies, child abuse and neglect, and childhood injuries has decreased.[23]

Home visiting programs are also cost-effective. In one study, by the time the children had reached the age of four, the government had saved $1,722 per child for the entire sample and $3,488 per child for low-income families. Savings were greatest in programs such as AFDC, Food Stamps, Medicaid, and Child Protective Services.[24]

The task force concluded that more intensive home visiting services should be made available to families who are at risk for poor maternal and child health outcomes. To be effective, these services should be

- Sensitive to family strengths, characteristics, and circumstances
- Comprehensive in focus, with multiple goals for both the mother and infant
- Geared to frequent visits that can extend flexibly over a one- or two-year period, depending on a families' needs
- Staffed by well-trained, properly supervised paraprofessionals and professionals, who have opportunities for continuing education

The task force agreed that these more comprehensive home visiting services would have the greatest benefit if offered to all families in communities with high rates of poverty and large numbers of single, young mothers. These voluntary services could help those most likely to benefit without singling out any particular mother or child in the neighborhood.

PROTECT YOUNG CHILDREN FROM INJURY AND PROMOTE THEIR HEALTH

Protect Young Children from Unintentional Injury

Despite modest decreases since 1912 in the overall rate of deaths from injury, unintentional injuries remain the leading cause of death among children aged one to four. While motor vehicle accidents predominate, deaths from fires, burns, drowning, and suffocation are particularly common among the very young.[25] Children growing up in poverty are more likely to die from an unintentional injury than children from better-off families.[26]

Patterns of childhood injury vary not only by income but also by gender and geography.[27] Males predominate as accident victims in all age groups, even among the very young. In 1988, for example, male babies accounted for 57 percent of the deaths from injury among those under one year of age; for children aged one to four, the figure was 61 percent. Death rates from house fires are similar for boys and girls, except between age two and four, when boys' tendency to play with matches and cigarette lighters may account for their higher

SAFEGUARDING CHILDREN

A napping baby sprawled on the back seat of a car; a toddler who picks at the paint on the kitchen wall and then eats it; an infant teething on a sharp-edged toy—they're all in danger. Many young children risk injury or illness all day long without venturing far from their normal routines.

The good news is that concerted efforts to childproof homes and reduce risks in the car and the neighborhood do work. Risk reduction requires parent education, so that new mothers and fathers (and other caregivers) can learn to spot possible hazards and prevent injuries; at the same time, policymakers, manufacturers, and community groups, must take a proactive approach to safeguarding children.

One effort to create injury-free environments for children is Communities for Child Safety, a program administered by the National 4-H Council. This program defines injury broadly to include intentional, unintentional, physical, and emotional harm. It brings together people who work in injury control and those who work in child abuse and neglect.

Begun in 1987 in Chicago, Communities for Child Safety sends two-person teams into neighborhoods to collect information on hazards, to develop networks with key organizations and support groups, to educate local residents, and to persuade local government and organizations to change their policies and approaches.

Teams urge communities to hold child safety fairs, to assess home safety, to offer infant/child CPR classes for parents, to educate parents in child safety, to establish fire safety programs, to work to prevent child abuse and neglect, and to clean up vacant lots and playgrounds. The goal is a community injury prevention plan.

death rate. Drowning deaths occur more often in states where there are large numbers of home swimming pools. Motor vehicle accident deaths are more common in less urban areas, where more families have cars and speed limits are higher.

While many childhood injuries do not result in death, they may result in disability or disfigurement and may compromise a child's

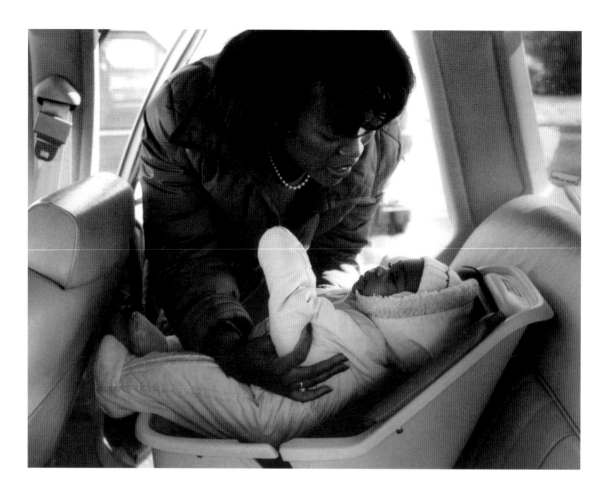

future development, well-being, and achievement. Because most of these injuries are preventable, the task force recommends new public strategies to reduce the incidence of unintentional injuries to young children. These strategies must include broad-based community efforts to encourage the use of child safety seats, fire alarms, window guards, and flame-retardant sleepwear, and to reduce the temperature of tap water in homes and child care settings.

Community-based prevention approaches are helpful, as shown by the National 4-H Council's Communities for Child Safety and other initiatives. In addition, a concerted effort is needed to educate parents and other adults about child protection. Leaders in health care, child care, government, social services, law enforcement, voluntary agencies, business and industry, construction and design, and the mass media can all contribute to making the preven-

tion of childhood injuries a national priority. The interests of very young children should be central in these efforts. Industry can develop nonflammable children's clothing and bedding; regulators and lawmakers can promote and enforce requirements to use car seats and to observe speed limits; engineers and architects can design new products or facilities that reduce the risk of injury for young children. The mass media can focus attention on young children and can provide information about products, risks, and methods of protection.[28]

Promote Children's Health
The task force concurs with other commissions that promoting young children's health is a responsibility shared by parents, other caregivers, the community, and health officials at

all levels of government.[29] Parents have the greatest responsibility for promoting healthy lifestyles at home and making certain their young children receive essential health care services: the mother's level of education and access to information are key determinants for children's health.[30] Other adults—child care workers, health providers, nonprofit agency and religious leaders, business, and the media—also have a responsibility to support families so that young children grow up physically and mentally healthy.

Child care providers can play a key role in promoting children's health and safety at home by creating a physical setting, preparing meals, and selecting toys that serve as models for parents. Child care staff can encourage parents to have their young children immunized (or can provide immunizations on site), can help them recognize illnesses or developmental difficulties, and can protect a child who may show signs of abuse or neglect. Health care providers can offer information about nutrition, child development, the parent–child relationship, and ways to childproof the house. Furthermore, both health care providers and child care staff can elicit support from other community members to develop community-based health education, injury prevention, and health care programs. These professionals can also sponsor activities and special projects to help families gain access to needed services.[31]

But how can we best support parents' own efforts to promote their children's health? First, community leaders can identify what needs to be known by parents and others in the community. Second, programs to teach health-promoting behaviors to parents can be started in accessible settings at convenient hours. Third, religious, civic, business, and other community organizations can communicate information

'ROAR' LAYS EARLY FOUNDATION FOR LITERACY

A Boston pediatrician tells the story of a harried young mother who arrives for her appointment with her toddler in tow. It's been a tough morning, and the afternoon promises to be no easier. In the waiting-room, an older woman approaches with an armload of books and asks if they would like a story.

The toddler takes an immediate interest, and the mother is struck by how many things he can name. She is surprised—and pleased—when the doctor later talks with her about sharing books with her toddler, and offers her a colorful book to take home. If the doctor is "prescribing" books, she reasons, it must be important.

This story is typical of the daily encounters in Reach Out and Read (ROAR), an innovative program at the Boston City Hospital that uses the pediatric visit to spark an interest in reading among families whose children are at risk for school failure. ROAR began in 1989 as a waiting-room program, because there parents and children are a captive audience, often for an extended period of time. ROAR provided volunteer adult readers, and found that young children were interested in the book and parents were intrigued by their children's behavior. ROAR considered the disappearance of children's books from the waiting room a positive sign. Today, ROAR offers assistance and resources to doctors and nurse practitioners, who then provide guidance to parents about reading and give them free children's books.

The program premise is that early cognitive experience is vital to later academic success. Among children served by the hospital, more than 25 percent experience significant reading delays and subsequent school problems; they are at increased risk for school failure. The psychological trauma that can follow school failure is often reflected in low self-esteem, teenage parenthood, delinquency, and substance abuse.

about children's health, setting as their highest priority the good health of every neighborhood child.[32]

CREATE SAFE ENVIRONMENTS FOR YOUNG CHILDREN

The public decries violent acts—child abuse, domestic violence, and murders—that take place in homes and neighborhoods. Although parents, community groups, and elected officials call for anticrime measures, the violence continues,[33] touching the life of too many children in this country—some more often and more directly than others. A child growing up in a poor community plagued by violence is also more likely to experience family violence, abuse, and neglect than a child from a more affluent community.[34]

Although most research and public debate about violence have focused on school-aged children and adolescents, violence also affects pregnant women, infants, and toddlers. Women face the highest risk of violence by a male partner during their childbearing years, and most particularly during pregnancy.[35] The abuse of pregnant women leads to serious risks for the infant, including low birthweight, birth defects, prematurity, and even such grave consequences as stillbirths and infant mortality.[36] After the baby is born, many abused women experience post-partum depression; consequently, their newborns often suffer from feeding problems and failure to thrive.[37]

OVERALL, REPEATED EXPOSURE TO VIOLENCE IS A THREAT TO CHILDREN'S HEALTHY PHYSICAL, INTELLECTUAL, AND EMOTIONAL DEVELOPMENT.

Very young children are also victims of abuse. Of the two million children who experience physical abuse or neglect each year, more than a third—some 700,000 in all—are infants under one year of age.[38] Premature infants are three times more likely than full-term infants to suffer abuse. When children under three years old are maltreated, the result is frequently permanent injury or death.[39] In 1990, almost 90 percent of those children who died as a result of abuse were under the age of five; 53 percent were less than a year old.[40]

The consequences for young children of community and familial violence has been little studied, but there is no doubt that they are adversely affected by such violence and that it interferes with their parents' ability to raise them. Indeed, during infancy and toddlerhood children should develop a sense of trust that the world is a safe place and that they are effective actors in that world. By the end of the first year, infants have a reasonable memory of important, major events that have particular meaning for them.[41] When the environment is not safe, children feel helpless and ineffective. Repeated exposure to violence affects children even before they have language. These children have difficulty sleeping and show increased anxiety and fearfulness. Young children withdraw, become depressed, and have difficulty paying attention. Overall, repeated exposure to violence is a threat to children's healthy physical, intellectual, and emotional development.

Parents, too, are affected by a climate of violence. Their ability to provide a safe environment is jeopardized when they must have their children play below the windowsills or

VIOLENCE AND CHILDREN: HOW COMMUNITIES HAVE RESPONDED

Today, there is growing awareness that young people who witness violence are also victims. In many parts of the country, young children are increasingly exposed to violence, both as the object of violence and as witnesses. Some communities are responding.

CHILD DEVELOPMENT AND COMMUNITY POLICING

The New Haven Department of Police Services, working with the Yale Child Study Center, has developed a program to provide

- Seminars for police officers on child development and human relationships
- A twenty-four-hour consultation service for children and families who have witnessed violence
- A weekly case conference for police and child mental health professionals

Called Child Development and Community Policing, the program has altered the ways in which police and mental health workers coordinate and deliver services to children and families exposed to violence. Police training emphasizes protection of the child's emotional and physical well-being. For example, police officers are trained to reunite children who have experienced traumatic violence with parents as quickly as possible and to call in clinicians immediately.

In the first year, the program trained all 450 members of the police department in the use of the consultation services; 150 officers attended seminars on child development and family functioning. In the first eighteen months of the consultation service, more than 300 children, ranging in age from two to seventeen, were referred by officers in the field. The children had been exposed to murders, stabbings, maiming by fire, death by drowning, and gunfire. They were seen individually or in groups in their homes, at police substations, and at the Child Study Center.

THE CHILD WITNESS TO VIOLENCE PROJECT

Children from birth to six who witness violence in their homes, between parents or other household members, and in the community, also need immediate attention. The Child Witness to Violence Project, started in 1992 at Boston City Hospital, identifies young children who have been exposed to violence and provides intervention to both the child and the family. The key to helping children is to support the adults who are most important to the child—whether parents, other relatives, or child care providers. Program therapists help these adults to cope with their own emotions so that they can shift their attention more quickly to the traumatized child.

LEADERSHIP TRAINING SEMINAR ON CHILDREN EXPOSED TO COMMUNITY VIOLENCE

Young children in Chicago commonly tell pediatric health care providers and teachers that they hear gunshots outside their homes, witness shootings on playgrounds in their neighborhoods, or have a relative who has been a victim or perpetrator of violence. In 1993, the Erikson Institute responded to requests for assistance from the community by providing an in-depth seminar series to enable professionals to help children, from birth to adolescence, and their parents cope with the effects of violence and trauma in their lives.

The project's goal is to help teachers of young children, child care staff, and community service professionals who work with families exposed to chronic violence to understand and respond more effectively to the families' special needs and concerns. Sixty professionals are taking part in the project. Seminars are held twice a month over a nine-month period; the sessions include information about how children view traumatic events, how better to intervene with these children in order to prevent long-term negative effects, and how to work with parents and other adults in the community. In addition, Erikson staff are available for on-site consultation and have developed a new workbook for children facing violence.

sleep in a bathtub to avoid random bullets, or when everyone knows a neighbor's child who has been killed or is a gang member. Parents often lose confidence and are so traumatized that they find it difficult to be emotionally responsive to their children.

The task force concludes that this nation must make a clear commitment to the right of all young children to grow up in safe homes and neighborhoods. Energy and resources must be directed toward preventing violence in children's lives and dealing with the damage that has already occurred. Two specific interventions seem warranted.

Adopt Family-Centered Approaches

Parents would benefit from family-centered approaches to help them understand the profound effects of violence—both in the family and in the community—on young children. Research indicates the strongest buffer for young children is a supportive relationship with parents. Most children are able to adjust to living in dangerous environments as long as their parents are not stressed beyond their capacity to cope.[42] Parent education and family support programs can help parents understand their critical role in the lives of their children. Parents must be taught skills in nonviolent conflict resolution and have access to proven programs that prevent child abuse and neglect.

In order to serve families best, support networks and individual counseling should be available to parents when necessary. The supporters themselves—the child care staff, health care professionals, counselors, religious leaders, and community workers—need more training in helping families and young children who are victims of violence. Parents themselves need to be able to contact these community resources to support and protect their children. Experts also need to develop a wide range of materials that describe positive parenting skills and offer ways to deal with acute and chronic trauma as they affect young children.

Initiate Community-Based Programs to Prevent Violence

In a growing number of communities today, parents consider few places to be safe and therefore restrict their children's play. Community programs to prevent violence help lower the levels of violence and increase the number of places that are safe for young children. For maximum effectiveness, such programs must be implemented locally, taking into account local conditions.

Increased funding must be made available for community programs that address violence prevention. For example, partnerships between child and family services and law enforcement agencies can support parents, help them develop positive behaviors, and work with families whose children are victims of violence. Such efforts convey to families that they are not alone, that society is committed to addressing violence in their communities.

Front-line workers need in-service consultation about how to deliver services in communities where violence is epidemic. Such efforts must coordinate child and family services with mental health professionals and law enforcement. Successful communitywide collaborations are already taking place in Boston, Chicago, New Haven, New Orleans, and Washington, D.C.

Central to ridding communities of violence is controlling access to guns. Citizens and policymakers have organized concerted, coordinated, and successful efforts to prevent drunk driving, to promote the use of seat belts, and to make smoking unacceptable. Similar efforts must occur with guns, especially given the power of the gun lobby. Even given enactment of the Brady law in late 1993, gun control laws in the United States have not effectively reduced the prevalence of guns in our society, but the American public's tolerance of guns is lessening. What is needed is nothing less than the removal of all guns, except those lawfully registered under stringent controls. Parents must be made to understand that possession of a gun for protection actually increases the chances of their children being injured or killed.[43] Clearly, however, before parents can accept this understanding and act on it, they must be confident that their communities are safe.

Appendix: Comprehensive Services Recommended for the Promotion of Child Health

In 1981, the Select Panel for the Promotion of Child Health, after a two-year study, identified the services necessary to ensure the health of America's chldren. The task force endorses the panel's recommendations and has updated them to reflect new medical developments.

Women of Reproductive Age

Services for nonpregnant women

Diagnosis and treatment of general health problems that can adversely affect future pregnancy, fetal development, and maternal health
- Sexually transmitted diseases
- Immune status (rubella, HIV)
- Gynecological anatomic and functional disorders
- Organic medical problems
- Nutritional status, including both over- and underweight
- Fertility and genetic problems
- Significant dental problems
- Occupational exposures
- Genetic risk

Diagnosis and treatment of mental health and behavioral problems
- Substance abuse, including alcohol
- Smoking cessation
- Significant mental disorders

Comprehensive family planning services
- Education and counseling
- Physical exam and lab tests
- Provision of family planning methods and instruction regarding their use
- Pregnancy testing, counseling and referrals as appropriate
- Infertility services and genetic testing
- Sterilization services

Home health and homemaker services

Prenatal services

Early diagnosis of pregnancy

Counseling for pregnancy continuation
- Referral to prenatal care
- Childbirth preparation classes
- Adoption
- Termination of pregnancy

Prenatal care
- History
- General physical exam
- Appropriate laboratory tests
- Diagnosis and treatment of general health problems
- Diagnosis and treatment of mental health problems
- Nutritional assessment and services
- Dental services
- Screening for infectious diseases
- Genetic screening, diagnosis, and counseling
- Identification and management of high-risk pregnancies

Counseling and anticipatory guidance regarding
- Physical activity and exercise
- Nutrition and adequate but not excessive weight gain during pregnancy
- Avoidance of substance abuse and environmental hazards
- Fetal growth and development and physiological changes in pregnancy
- Signs of abnormal pregnancy and of the onset of labor
- Preparation for labor (including partner, where appropriate)
- Use of medications during pregnancy
- Infant nutritional needs and feeding practices, including breastfeeding
- Child care arrangements
- Parenting skills, including risk of child abuse or neglect
- Linkage to continuous and comprehensive pediatric care
- Emotional and social changes brought on by the birth of a child

Perinatal and postpartum care

Monitoring labor

Medical services during labor and delivery

Delivery by qualified professional in a facility with adequate services

Diagnosis and treatment of general health problems

Diagnosis and treatment of mental health and behavior problems (postpartum depression)

Counseling and anticipatory guidance regarding

- Infant development and behavior
- Infant nutrition and feeding, including breastfeeding
- Home and automobile accident prevention
- Infant stimulation and parenting skills, including risk of abuse or neglect
- Immunization
- Health-damaging behavior by parents, including substance abuse and smoking
- Continuous and comprehensive health care
- Recognition and management of illness in the newborn
- Hygiene and first aid
- Child care arrangements
- Other relevant topics of patient concern

HEALTH EDUCATION

Counseling and anticipatory guidance, as listed above

Developing positive health habits

Using health services appropriately

Accessing community health and social services

ACCESS-RELATED SERVICES

Transportation as appropriate

- Emergency transport
- Transportation services associated with a regionalized perinatal or tertiary care network
- Transportation services that facilitate obtaining needed health services

Outreach services

Hotline, translator, and 24-hour emergency telephone services

Child care services to facilitate obtaining needed health services

INFANTS UNDER ONE YEAR

SERVICES IN THE NEONATAL PERIOD

Evaluation and support immediately after delivery

Complete physical exam

Laboratory tests to screen for genetic disease and thyroid function

Diagnosis and treatment of general health problems, both acute and chronic

Preventive procedures, including

- Gonococcal eye infection prophylaxis
- Administration of vitamin K

Services of a neonatal intensive care unit, as appropriate

Nutritional assessment and supplementation, as needed

Bonding, attachment support, and extended contact with parents, including rooming-in, if desired

Linkage to continuous and comprehensive pediatric care after discharge

Home health services

Be alert for signs of abuse and neglect

SERVICES FOR CHILDREN

Periodic health assessment, including

- History and systems review
  - Medical history
  - Social setting
  - Family background
  - Genetic assessment
  - Age and development stage
  - Potential problems
- Complete physical examination, including
  - Height and weight
  - Head circumference
  - Developmental/behavioral assessment
  - Vision and hearing evaluation
- Screening and laboratory tests as indicated, including
  - Hemoglobin/hematocrit
  - Tuberculin skin test
  - Lead poisoning
  - Parasites
  - Screening for sickle cell and other disorders of hemoglobin
- Nutritional assessment and supplementation, as needed, including
  - Iron
  - Vitamin D
  - Fluoride

Immunizations

continued on page 82

Diagnosis and treatment of general health problems, both acute and chronic

Home health services

SERVICES FOR FAMILIES DURING INFANT'S FIRST YEAR

Counseling and anticipatory guidance regarding

- Infant development and behavior
- Maternal nutritional needs, especially if breastfeeding
- Infant nutritional needs and feeding practices
- Home and automobile accident prevention
- Infant stimulation and parenting skills, including risk of abuse or neglect
- Immunizations
- Health-damaging behavior by parents, including substance abuse and smoking
- Continuous and comprehensive health care
- Recognition and management of illness
- Hygiene and first aid
- Child care arrangements
- Other relevant issues in response to parental concern

Counseling and appropriate treatment or referral as needed for parents

- Who have chronic health problems that affect their capacity to care for the infant, including
  - Handicapping conditions
  - Substance-abuse problems
  - Mental health problems (including maternal depression)
- Whose infant in seriously ill
- Whose infant has a chronic illness or a handicapping condition
- Whose infant is or is about to be hospitalized

HEALTH EDUCATION

Counseling and anticipatory guidance, as listed above

Developing positive health habits

Using health services appropriately

Accessing community health and social services

ACCESS-RELATED SERVICES

Transportation as appropriate

- Emergency transport
- Transportation services associated with a regionalized perinatal or tertiary care network
- Transportation services that facilitate obtaining needed health services

Outreach services

Hotline, translator, and 24-hour emergency telephone services

Child care services to facilitate obtaining needed health services

CHILDREN FROM ONE YEAR TO THREE YEARS

SERVICES FOR CHILDREN

Periodic health assessment, including

- History and systems review
  - Medical history
  - Social setting
  - Family background
  - Genetic assessment
  - Age and developmental stage
  - Potential problems
- Psychosocial history
  - Peer and family relationships
  - Child care progress and problems
- Complete physical examination
  - Height and weight
  - Developmental and behavioral assessment
  - Vision, hearing, and speech evaluation
  - Signs of abuse and neglect
- Screening and laboratory tests as indicated, including

- Hemoglobin/hematocrit
- Tuberculin skin test
- Lead poisoning
- Parasites
- Screening for sickle cell and other hemoglobin disorders
- Nutritional assessment and supplementation, as needed, including iron, vitamin D, and fluoride

Immunizations

Diagnosis and treatment of general health problems, both acute and chronic

Diagnosis and treatment of mental health disorders, both acute and chronic
- Emotional disorders
- Learning disorders
- Behavioral disorders
- Substance abuse
- Problems with family and peer group

Counseling and support services for children with chronic or handicapping conditions

Dental services, preventive and therapeutic

Home health services

SERVICES FOR CHILDREN AND THEIR FAMILIES
Counseling and anticipatory guidance regarding
- Nutritional needs
- Home and automobile injury prevention
- Parenting skills, including risk of abuse or neglect
- Immunizations
- Health-damaging behavior by parents, including substance abuse and smoking
- Continuous and comprehensive health care
- Child care arrangements
- Physical activity and exercise
- Hygiene and first aid
- Dental health

- Childhood antecedents of adult illness
- Child development
- Environmental hazards
- Other relevant issues in response to child and parental concern

Counseling and appropriate treatment or referral, as needed, for parents
- Who have chronic health problems that affect their capacity to care for the child, including
  - Handicapping conditions
  - Substance-abuse problems
  - Mental health problems (including maternal depression)
- Whose child is seriously ill
- Whose child has a chronic illness or a handicapping condition
- Whose child is or is about to be hospitalized

HEALTH EDUCATION
Counseling and anticipatory guidance, as listed above

Developing positive health habits

Using health services appropriately

Accessing social services and entitlements

ACCESS-RELATED SERVICES
Transportation as appropriate
- Emergency transport
- Transportation services associated with a regionalized or tertiary care network
- Transportation services that facilitate obtaining needed health services

Outreach services

Hotline, translator, and 24-hour emergency telephone services

Child care services to facilitate obtaining needed health services

MOBILIZE COMMUNITIES TO SUPPORT YOUNG CHILDREN AND THEIR FAMILIES

T ake a walk around the neighborhood, virtually any neighborhood, in the late morning, when most Americans are at school or work. That's when infants and toddlers seem to be out in force—lifted from car seat to shopping cart, carried or wheeled down Main Street, or set loose in a sandbox. The adults who care for them have ventured out to do errands, visit the doctor, calm a fussy baby, or perhaps just to escape the isolation of solitary child care. Some find themselves in communities that respond to their needs and those of their children. Town centers have sidewalks for strolling, and the kinds of playgrounds and parks where children can safely play and adults can comfortably sit. Stores and restaurants welcome people with infants and toddlers, shopping malls accommodate small children, and family drop-in centers provide a meeting place—a source of stimulation for the children and of information and social contact for adults. Essential services, like clinics or pharmacies, are conveniently located, and have hours that make sense for working parents. In short, the community's institutions, both public and private, are designed in ways that weave young children and their caregivers into the social fabric.

But those communities are the exception rather than the rule. More often, outings into the community can be stressful, frustrating events for people with infants and toddlers. Most communities are far more responsive to the needs of their "working" residents—those who hold jobs outside the home and who do not have small children—than to the needs of adults caring for small children. This is no accident. For the most part, new parents tend to have less influence than other community members: overwhelmed and isolated by the demands of home and work responsibilities, they often have less financial clout, less involvement in community affairs, and less say in setting priorities.

A Community that Supports Families with Young Children

This report identifies four key starting points for young children that may also serve as starting points for community planning. To support families with young children, a community must invest its human and financial resources to

- **Support parent education:** Encourage parents to make responsible choices in planning to have children; make family planning and prenatal health care services widely available; and educate parents and all community members about the importance of good parenting.
- **Broaden quality child care options:** Give all parents access to quality, affordable child care options, so that they can nurture their children while pursuing economic self-sufficiency and personal growth. Quality child care and parental leave are essential choices that all parents need.
- **Guarantee adequate health care:** Provide parents and their children with comprehensive primary and preventive health care, and educate parents and community-based providers about injury prevention to ensure safe and protective environments for children.
- **Strengthen community networks:** Draw together community programs to establish accessible and welcoming neighborhood and child family centers so that all parents can get the support they need in raising their young children.

For these and other reasons, the community services available to most families with children under age three are few and fragmentary. When a new baby joins a family, relatives, friends, and neighbors may pitch in, keeping an eye on older children, offering advice about calming a colicky infant, or bringing over a casserole. But new parents need more systematic, sustained support. Families of all kinds need help in balancing childrearing and workplace responsibilities, in acquiring the best possible child care and health care, and in dealing with the inevitable stress of raising a young child—often without the support of an extended family.

The bottom line is this: most communities do not adequately support a healthy start for our youngest children, and our nation has not mobilized the resources or the will to meet their needs. This is the quiet crisis that threatens the stability of community and family life across this nation.

COMMUNITIES COUNT

Reversing the quiet crisis requires more than the provision of direct services to families, such as those described in preceding chapters. It has become increasingly clear that we also need to support communities so that they in turn can strengthen family life.

A growing body of research supports the premise, most eloquently formulated more than half a century ago in the work of L. S. Vygotsky, that human development, and especially cognitive growth, occurs in the context of engagement in joint activities with important people in our lives, both relatives and nonrelatives. Recent studies extend this notion by exploring the role of neighborhoods and communities in mediating broad cultural, social, and economic forces and thereby molding the lives of families and children. These studies demonstrate that supportive social networks help parents to utilize community resources, to cope with stress, and to learn new parenting styles. They show that neighborhood characteristics do indeed affect individual outcomes for children.[1]

Ecology and Children

Two strands of community-level research are especially relevant to the work of the task force. The first takes an *ecological* approach to improving children's chances of getting a secure, healthy start in life. The term "ecological" suggests that a viable, sustainable habitat is crucial to the survival of a species. Applied to child development, the ecological approach assumes that a family's effectiveness as a childrearing system is bolstered by the existence of a supportive social network that includes people outside the immediate family—relatives, friends, neighbors, coworkers, and other community members. In short, it assumes that as we raise our children, communities count.[2]

Before the late seventies, researchers paid relatively little attention to this approach. They tended to view personal networks as private matters, since they grew out of extended family relationships and individual friendships. But there is growing evidence that the kinds of social networks developed by parents, and later by the children themselves, have an impact on children's mental and physical well-being and on their success in school.

One large study followed 160 families in ten neighborhoods of Syracuse, New York: it included families with a wide range of ethnic, economic, and structural characteristics. Over a three-year period, families took part in a Child and Family Neighborhood Program that provided a variety of resources that supported parents' childrearing efforts. The program did not explicitly aim to expand parents' social contacts, but researchers did study the development and effects of these networks. The study showed that when parents are more connected to other families in their communities,

THE COMMUNITY SERVICES AVAILABLE TO
MOST FAMILIES WITH CHILDREN UNDER AGE
THREE ARE FEW AND FRAGMENTARY.

their children benefit. Stronger, larger networks had a positive effect on parents' ability to deal with stress, on mothers' perceptions of themselves and their children, on fathers' involvement in childrearing, and on children's self-esteem and school success. In addition, the researchers found that, in some circumstances, network resources reduced the probability of certain mental and physical illnesses.[3]

Social Disorganization: Children Pay the Price

A second line of research comes from social disorganization theory—the study of the way people are affected by the degree of social organization in their neighborhoods. It focuses not only on the community's formal institutions, but also on its informal networks—the density of acquaintanceships, the ties among different generations within extended families, and the shared responsibility for children. It suggests that when people feel responsible for what happens in their neighborhoods, children benefit.

Moreover, this research shows that the absence of social cohesion can have a devastating effect on the entire community, but particularly on its youngest members. In particular, it suggests that social disorganization, in combination with urban poverty, can lead to low birthweight, child abuse and neglect, cognitive impairment, and adjustment problems. Researchers have found that social isolation not only deprives parents of crucial resources; it also limits their access to the kind of cultural learning and positive role models that can help them cope better at home, in school, and on the job. And finally, they suggest that commu-

nity-level interventions to provide prenatal care, to promote infant and child health, to impart childrearing skills, and to teach conflict resolution are promising.[4]

Helping Families by Improving Community Supports

These findings strengthen the task force's conviction that families can benefit from improved community supports—in particular, when communities are able to develop a broad, coherent approach that makes sense for their population of families with children under age three. This is a daunting challenge, requiring the good ideas and hard work of people across the nation: government officials, business leaders, agency staff, community workers, and volunteers. But the long-term payoffs will be substantial. A good start in life measurably decreases the risk that individuals will drop out of school, swell the welfare rolls, or shuttle in and out of the criminal justice system. All of society clearly benefits when young children grow up to be productive, secure, active citizens.

PROMOTE A CULTURE OF RESPONSIBILITY

The task force recommends that every community in America focus attention on the needs of children under three and their families, beginning in the prenatal period. We urge leaders to marshal resources on their behalf, to learn from effective, innovative models, to plan carefully, and to measure and report the results of these efforts to the public. Because many American families with young children face multiple risk factors—including poverty, unemployment, inadequate housing, and violence—we recommend that special attention be given to services and supports that benefit those most in need.

SETTING GOALS FOR EFFECTIVE
COMMUNITY PLANNING

By undertaking a comprehensive assessment or "audit" of the status of families with children under the age of three, a community-based planning group can document not only a community's problems, but also its strengths. During the planning process, this group should actively encourage public input and discussion in a variety of community forums. Reports summarizing major findings should be issued periodically to inform the community, inspire voluntary commitment, and influence public policy.

During the planning process, the group should

- Gather data that answer basic questions about the characteristics and needs of families with young children, including their numbers, geographic distribution, income, family composition, ethnicity and race, and environmental risks. What trends are observable over the past several years?

- Interview parents, program staff, service providers, and public school teachers to pinpoint key challenges in their particular community.

- Determine the scope and accessibility of services and supports now available to families, including family planning, parenting and family life education, child care, and pre- and postnatal health care.

- Analyze the public and private sector policies that affect parents' ability to balance work and family commitments.

- Survey community resources available to families with young children, including housing, parks, libraries, recreation and drop-in centers, health care and child care facilities, voluntary agencies, places of worship, and informal assistance.

- Establish clear goals and priorities, and recommend interventions that meet those goals.

- Create an ongoing mechanism to monitor the implementation of its recommendations.

- Throughout the process, promote collaboration among the many institutions and individuals who work with families and young children.

One community that has pulled together a promising planning process for meeting the needs of families with young children is Austin, Texas. Launched in 1992, the Austin Project seeks to mobilize the public and private sectors to reverse the decline of several inner-city neighborhoods. Arguing that conditions for families, children, and youth pose "not only a profound moral problem but also heavy, rising costs and a threat to the future workforce of Austin," Professors Walt and Elspeth Rostow of the Lyndon B. Johnson School of Public Affairs at the University of Texas, organized a multisectoral group, including the mayor of Austin, a county court judge, the president of the local school board, and church, corporate, and community leaders. In September 1992, the group produced a report entitled *An Investment Plan for the Young*, documenting its goals and principles. The report states that "a strategy of continuous support and widened opportunity for families and children at every stage of life from prenatal care to entry into the workforce must be developed."

To achieve its goals, the Austin Project developed a five-year financial and capacity-building plan, identifying the care of children from before birth to age eight as the community's "most pressing priority." The plan states: "It is a vital interest of the whole Austin community that every baby born in our city be given a healthy start in life."

The Austin five-year plan includes measurable goals and specific progress benchmarks, including reduction of the infant mortality rate and of the incidence of low-birthweight babies; increase in the use of nutrition programs by pregnant women; better primary health care coverage for infants and toddlers; reduction of preventable injuries; improvement of child care quality through better provider training; and availability of parent education, information, and support to all families.

A sustained, systematic effort of this kind requires broad-based action at the local level, the commitment and imagination of service providers, the spirited involvement of Americans from all walks of life, and the support of state and national government. Without all these constituencies on board, communities will not be able to develop the "culture of responsibility" needed to institute real change.

Need for Local Leadership

At the same time, we recognize that leadership for change must be local. The problems of young children and their families do not lend themselves to one-size-fits-all solutions. Communities need to develop their own approaches to creating family-centered communities, based on a strategic planning process that involves all sectors of the community: parent and neighborhood groups, government, business, voluntary agencies, health and child care providers, the school system, the media, and religious institutions.

This kind of broad-based effort demands strong local leadership—a core of change agents who have strong community ties and sufficient flexibility to reach consensus on goals. In some communities, a citizens group or a private/public partnership may already be addressing issues of education, health care, or family services, and can broaden or refocus its agenda to address the specific needs of very young children and their families. In other communities, forming such a group will be the first step.

THE BOTTOM LINE IS THIS: MOST COMMUNITIES DO NOT ADEQUATELY SUPPORT A HEALTHY START FOR OUR YOUNGEST CHILDREN.

Community Assessments

The process should begin with a community assessment, examining the needs of young children and families, especially those with multiple risk factors, and the capacity of existing programs to meet those needs.[5] Planners must ask such questions as

- What kinds of preparation for parenthood, parent education and support, and family planning services are available? Who is benefiting from them?
- What kinds of prenatal care are available, and how many expectant mothers do they reach?
- How much infant and toddler child care is available in the community, and what is its quality?
- What proportion of young children in the community receive the full recommended course of immunizations?
- Which public and voluntary agencies serve families with children under age three? Are they meeting local needs? To what extent are their services coordinated?
- Which factors and resources in the community promote or inhibit the development of social networks among families with young children?
- What funds are available from public and private sources? How are they being expended to serve families with young children? How can we improve funding mechanisms and achieve greater cost-effectiveness?
- What additional resources can be leveraged from business, volunteers, and the private, nonprofit sector?

NEW PARTNERSHIPS FOR COMMUNITY INNOVATION

Increasingly, foundations, entrepreneurial investment funds, and civic groups are responding to the problems of families with young children by forming public–private partnerships to support innovative, community-based solutions. Three examples are particularly noteworthy.

• **The Children's Initiative:** In 1991, the Pew Charitable Trusts, one of the nation's largest private philanthropies, established "The Children's Initiative"—a major grant-making program designed to demonstrate how to improve the lives of families with young children on a broad scale. The foundation has made a large multiyear commitment to help states and communities adopt "a new way of working with families, to reshape service delivery systems, and to make the investments necessary to shift from a crisis-oriented, fragmented, and inadequate approach to one of inclusion and effective supports for all children."

The Pew Trusts are working intensively in communities in five states: Kentucky, Florida, Georgia, Minnesota, and Rhode Island. Each state has organized a high-level leadership group and has developed a comprehensive plan to achieve four critical outcomes: improved child health, good child development, reduced barriers to school performance, and better family functioning and stability. Each plan will gauge progress toward these goals in terms of specific measures, such as a reduced rate of infant mortality and reduced incidence of child abuse and neglect.

• **The Ounce of Prevention Fund:** The Chicago-based Ounce of Prevention Fund is an example of a new kind of organization that draws upon family, community, and government resources to promote the well-being of children and adolescents. Established in 1982 and initially financed with both state and private monies, the fund broke new ground in collaborative models. The fact that it is a private–public partnership improves the fund's leverage with government: support has come not only from dozens of corporations and individuals, but also from the U.S. Department of Health and Human Services and several state agencies.

The collaboration also frees the Ounce of Prevention Fund to innovate. The result is a strong network of programs, research, and advocacy for children, youth, and families in Illinois. The fund also operates the much-publicized Center for Successful Child Development in the Robert Taylor Homes in Chicago, the nation's largest high-rise public housing development. The center provides services and supports to families and their children in an environment that many observers consider to be the worst public housing conditions in the United States.

• **Kiwanis Club Programs:** Established civic groups are also supporting child-oriented programs. Kiwanis International has designated young children "Priority One," and has asked each of its five thousand clubs to develop a project addressing maternal and infant health, child care and development, parent education and support, or safety and pediatric trauma.

The resulting projects range from building a playground for a child care center to distributing a safety brochure (translated into ten languages) throughout Europe. Some clubs distribute books to preschoolers, and others offer community education about shaken baby syndrome. Several clubs have developed videotapes, printed materials, or project ideas that have been shared with other clubs. Kiwanis divisions and districts have launched larger efforts, including immunization programs and the establishment of pediatric trauma centers.

Eliminate Weaknesses and Build on Strengths

As they look at existing resources, communities are likely to find that some programs are effective, or would be with relatively minor adjustments. It is important not to dismantle programs that work or to disrupt networks that have been painstakingly established.

Other programs will prove to be less effective. Many are understaffed. In other cases, staff members may not have the educational background or sufficient training to plan activities for children that are developmentally appropriate, to work effectively with families, or to make appropriate referrals to other services.

Perhaps the most serious weakness the community planning process will uncover is insufficient coordination among programs serving the same families.[6] Forging links among these programs should be a top priority. Parent education programs will be more effective if they are linked to family planning and employment/training services. Child care programs can serve children better if they link parents to family service agencies that can help them cope with their many responsibilities and to neighborhood schools to ensure a smooth transition as children move on.

These linkages provide a more comprehensive, family-centered system of supports for young children and their families. They can also result in a shared information system, making it unnecessary for parents to tell the same story over and over again to different professionals in different agencies. And most important, this comprehensive system can help to seal the cracks through which many young children now slip.

Once services are linked, decision makers are in a better position to eliminate duplication of services, and to see where new services can be added or existing services modified. The process may result in more efficient delivery mechanisms. For example, a van can deliver both medical and parent education services to hard-to-reach mothers in high-risk neighborhoods.

Emphasizing Results

Once the assessment is completed and documented, the leadership group needs to reach consensus on goals, and to define the specific interventions that will meet those goals. A strong plan will probably include elements that benefit families with young children directly (such as prenatal care programs or parent education services) and those that benefit them indirectly by reinforcing social cohesion within the community (such as improving community safety, which makes it possible for parents to gather).

A key challenge at this stage is establishing credibility by building program performance measures into these plans. These measures would define quantitative and qualitative results. An emphasis on results is crucial for several reasons:

- It focuses attention on what children and families in a particular community need (such as the reduction of infant mortality, more accessible child care, or higher immunization rates) and on how those needs were met, rather than on the number of services provided or the number of people served.[7]

- It promotes communitywide efforts on behalf of children. As individuals and agencies with different professional orientations work together, they must define and agree on shared goals. Collaborative relationships are strengthened, and a communitywide culture of responsibility is nurtured.

- It may help restore public confidence that financial investments are paying off. Opinion polls show that the many citizens who have lost confidence in government and other institutions will support new investments in human services only when they are convinced that the investment is producing the promised results.

> AS INDIVIDUALS AND AGENCIES WITH DIFFERENT PROFESSIONAL ORIENTATIONS WORK TOGETHER, THEY MUST DEFINE AND AGREE ON SHARED GOALS.

MOVE TOWARD FAMILY-CENTERED COMMUNITIES

The task force envisions a strategic planning process that would move communities toward a family-centered approach—a cluster of resources and services linked together so that more parents can, with efficiency and dignity, gain access to essential information and services and fulfill their responsibilities to their young children.

SCHOOLS OF THE 21ST CENTURY
LINK SERVICES FOR FAMILIES

Services to families with young children can thrive in many different settings. Many communities are beginning to realize the potential of the neighborhood public school as the hub in a network of programs serving children under three and their families. As a physical plant, the public school is often under-utilized, and its location is usually convenient and well known. And most residents have a sense of ownership of the school; they know that their taxes have paid for it. But until recently, most parents never ventured into schools until their children approached the age of five.

Today, we are moving toward an expanded understanding of the public school's mission that is rooted in the nation's first education goal: school readiness. To attain this goal, education leaders are seeking ways to reach families and children long before they enter kindergarten.

An increasingly popular school-based model that links community programs for families with young children is Schools of the 21st Century. Developed at Yale University, this program reaches out to expectant parents through linkages with parent education and family support programs such as Parents as Teachers.

Here's how it works: Parents enroll voluntarily in a home visiting program that ensures that, from the moment a pregnancy is known, appropriate information, advice, and services are available. To help parents locate quality child care, for example, program staff make referrals to a network of family child care homes and child care centers in the community. A school resource center also provides linkages to health, nutrition, and other services that parents may need during the first three years of their child's life. Once the child turns three, the family can obtain quality child care at the school site. Before- and after-school child care and educational enrichment programs are available for children aged five to twelve.

A resource center at the school, staffed by individuals certified in early childhood education, provides ongoing professional development for teachers, home visitors, and other community providers.

The program is financed through parent fees, government sponsorship, and private donations. Schools of the 21st Century have been successfully implemented in many parts of the nation, including Connecticut, Missouri, Texas, Mississippi, Virginia, and Wyoming.

Each community or neighborhood would develop a network of services geared to the needs of its families. This network of services can and will take many forms, reflecting and reinforcing the informal social supports that are already in place. But we anticipate that in each community, a single institution would become the center of the network, offering support, information, and referrals to families and providers. This institution would become known in the community as the place parents can turn to for information, advice, or service—an institution so useful and so accessible that parents and community leaders will wonder how they ever got along without it.

This recommendation reflects a growing interest in family-centered comprehensive programs. Several recent studies show how a network of comprehensive programs for families with young children serves the needs of different communities. These studies conclude that, unlike traditional services, many centers help to prevent crises by responding early and flexibly to the needs of families and communities; by reaching out to families, including those that social service bureaucracies often miss; and by emphasizing family strengths rather than weaknesses. They are user-friendly, creating home-like settings or offering services in families' homes.[8]

Create Neighborhood Family and Child Centers

The task force encourages broad experimentation with a comprehensive approach through the development of neighborhood family and child centers. We encourage collaboration with local colleges and universities so that we can move expertise on child development from campuses to communities; and with local businesses and agencies, so that we can move expertise on program management from board rooms to play rooms.

As these centers evolve, they can move toward providing a full spectrum of services, including:

- Parent education and ongoing support groups
- One-stop access to information about child care, schools, health care, social services, and a wide range of other community resources
- Outreach to families with multiple risk factors
- Professional development and technical assistance for caregivers and service providers

Some communities may establish new family and child centers; others may choose to expand an existing program at a neighborhood drop-in center, preschool, health facility, library, settlement house, religious institution, or community agency. In fact, a family and child center could be built on any credible community institution and could be financed through the expansion and redirection of government funds, private support, and parent fees. Each community should establish its own strategy for administering these centers, but it is essential that parents and other neighborhood residents be involved in their development and management.

Communities and states throughout the nation are experimenting with a wide range of comprehensive programs for families with young children, including Parent–Child Centers, Schools of the 21st Century, Smart Start, Healthy Start, Better Babies, Success by Six, Avance, and Parents as Teachers. Committed to the best of American pluralism and entrepreneurship, the task force encourages broad variation in the implementation of local programs.

Expand Head Start

In many communities, however, existing Head Start programs are a logical starting point for the provision of comprehensive services and supports for infants and toddlers and their families. Since 1965, Head Start has combined developmentally oriented child care with community involvement, support of parents, and provision of nutrition, health care, and social services. Historically, Head Start has had a limited mandate: it has served primarily three- to five-year-old children from low-income families who need an extra boost to be ready for school. And like many large-scale programs, it has been criticized at times for uneven quality. But on the whole, Head Start has gained enormous credibility as a cost-effective, national program that significantly improves chances of early school success.

Head Start now serves some 700,000 three- to five-year-olds each year. But in 1992, Head Start served only one out of every twenty economically eligible children under age three. In the 1990s, when the nation has become committed to school success for all, and when we have learned that the fundamental building

A FAMILY AND CHILD CENTER COULD BE BUILT ON ANY CREDIBLE COMMUNITY INSTITUTION AND COULD BE FINANCED THROUGH GOVERNMENT FUNDS, PRIVATE SUPPORT, AND PARENT FEES.

A HEAD START MODEL FOR THE UNDER-THREES

In 1966, a federal government task force established by President Johnson recommended the development of a comprehensive service program for families with children under three years of age. Known as Parent–Child Centers, this initiative was conceived as a key element of the newly established Head Start program. Originally, thirty-six sites were established in thirty states and the District of Columbia, but the program was virtually eliminated in the 1970s. Since that time it has grown slowly; in 1992 there were 106 centers serving fewer than 20,000 infants and toddlers.

Many of the existing centers may act as models for Head Start services for the "under–threes." One strong program is the Edward C. Mazique Parent–Child Center, which operates in one of our nation's poorest neighborhoods, not far from the United States Capitol in Washington, D.C. The Mazique Center serves more than 500 families on a regular basis: 75 percent are African American; the remainder are predominantly Hispanic. The center provides comprehensive, integrated services and collaborates extensively with other neighborhood programs. Its primary features are

- *Home-Based Program.* Beginning during pregnancy, home visitors provide information and referrals relating to prenatal care, nutrition, parenting styles, and child development. The program supports parents in their child-rearing responsibilities until their child enters kindergarten.

- *Quality Child Care.* Once their child reaches the age of six weeks, parents can obtain high-quality center-based child care provided by well-trained staff in a developmentally appropriate program. After the child's second birthday, parents may chose a preschool child care program with longer hours, or the child may remain in the center-based child care setting. In either case, the child will enter a Head Start program at age three. Family involvement is actively encouraged.

- *An Emphasis on Adolescent Parents.* The "junior parents" program is designed for adolescent parents (ages 13–18) and their families. The program encourages adolescents to remain in school by providing high-quality child care for children between six weeks and three years of age, and by supporting and guiding the parents' own educational, career, and personal options.

- *Early Intervention for Children with Special Needs.* The center provides a multiservice approach for children from six weeks to five years of age with moderate to severe developmental delays or diagnosed disabilities. The program includes assessment, therapy, and transportation.

The center provides other important services, including an onsite pediatric medical clinic, career development and job training, social services, drug treatment, crisis intervention counseling, and resource and referral services. It is also engaged in research and development activities.

blocks of school learning must be in place long before children reach Head Start age, that is not enough.[9]

In light of new research and experience, the task force concludes that Head Start (and similar programs) must begin much earlier. Although Head Start services have been offered primarily to disadvantaged children, the program's emphasis on healthy development is a sound and effective starting point for every American family.

We recommend that the comprehensive, family-friendly and community-based services that have characterized Head Start now be expanded to provide appropriate services and supports for younger children and to be a source of consistent support between the pre-natal period and school entry. Beginning with the most disadvantaged families, the new program for children under three should include home visits, immunizations, linkages to prenatal and other health care, parent education and support, and developmentally sound child care, as well as nutrition and social services. These would equip parents to be the effective first teachers of their young children, and could link up with adult job training, drug treatment, housing, and economic development programs. Head Start programs for younger children could be associated with schools, settlement houses, existing Head Start programs, or other community institutions.

This recommendation furthers the conclusions of the Advisory Committee on Head Start Quality and Expansion, formed in 1993 by the secretary of health and human services. The advisory committee's report envisions an expanded and renewed Head Start that serves as a central community institution, but the report emphasizes that the quality of services must be a first priority. The advisory committee's recommendations for enhancing quality by focusing on staffing and career development, improving local program management, bolstering federal oversight, providing better facilities, and strengthening the role of research must apply to program expansion for families with children under age three.

In expanding its services to children under age three, Head Start should ensure that every aspect of the program, particularly staffing, is appropriate for infants and toddlers and their families. In particular, Head Start needs to establish performance standards geared to the specific needs of infants and toddlers; to involve people trained in early childhood development and health in the oversight process; and to strengthen professional development and technical assistance for local programs.

If these quality issues are addressed, an expanded Head Start could give new energy and new hope to the many committed individuals and organizations now struggling to ensure that all children might will be ready for school and could brighten the future of those children who might otherwise fall behind.

REINVENT GOVERNMENT

As things stand, families with young children are confronted by a fragmented, unwieldy array of services—the result of government-sponsored programs launched in response to narrowly defined problems or to the circumscribed needs of particular populations. As one report notes, "what we have now is a largely uncoordinated array of programs and providers struggling to deliver services without any vision or systematic support to ensure quality and efficiency."[10]

To spark community change that will benefit families with children under three, federal and state governments must help communities improve their services and supports. They can do so by mounting systematic efforts to support local change, by removing obstacles created by outmoded funding patterns and cumbersome regulations, and by mobilizing other sectors, including business and the media, to make the needs of families with young children a high priority.

Promote Federal Leadership

In order to focus the leadership and resources of the federal government much more sharply on the needs of young children and their families, the task force recommends the following steps:

- *Establish high-level federal planning to promote state and local initiatives.* We recommend that the President direct a high-level federal group to coordinate federal agency support for young children and families.
- *Develop consistent federal policy that encourages experimentation.* To facilitate effective planning, this high-level federal group should compile a full inventory of the specific obstacles that states and local communities encounter in their efforts to use federal funds to provide more effective services and supports to families with young children. The cabinet should grant selective waivers from federal and state regulations or mandates, where appropriate, to permit innovation at the local level.

> AS THINGS STAND, FAMILIES WITH YOUNG CHILDREN ARE CONFRONTED BY A FRAGMENTED, UNWIELDY ARRAY OF SERVICES.

- *Ensure the adequacy, coherence, and coordination of federal programs for families with young children.* Several recent federal initiatives, including Part H of the Individuals with Disabilities Education Act, the Comprehensive Child Development Program, and the Family Preservation and Support Services Program, represent departures from narrow categorical funding and fragmented service delivery. The model provided by Part H for young children with disabilities, though inadequately funded, offers important guidance because its key feature requires that every child eligible for assistance must receive an individualized, comprehensive service plan. The expansion of Head Start to serve younger children, as described above, is another essential step.

State Councils Lead Action for Families and Young Children

Today, a growing number of states are emphasizing early childhood development as a significant new "front-end" investment. Most states have embraced the importance of getting children "ready for school" and are now emphasizing ways to prevent social, health, and educational problems before they have serious and costly consequences. State coordinating councils can be an effective way to focus resources and attention on these issues. With sustained gubernatorial or legislative leadership, a state council can provide impetus for community action.

In 1987, Colorado's governor Roy Romer established a pioneering early childhood initiative called "First Impressions." The initiative's purpose was to ensure that all of Colorado's children enter kindergarten ready to learn. The state has developed a comprehensive plan and has established statewide and community councils. The initiative takes advantage of the public education power of Colorado's First Lady, Bea Romer, who has attended numerous community events and meetings. Technical assistance is provided to local communities to help them develop new programs, pool existing funding to achieve better results, and build local leadership capacity among parents and advocates.

The governor has also created a Families and Children Cabinet Council that has broad authority over program planning for young children. The group consists of high-level representatives from the departments of education, social services, health, and mental health. As part of Colorado's Strategic Plan for Families and Children, neighborhood family centers that combine health, education, and human services in a single location are now being established. Local planning teams select the programs and services to be offered at the center and work with state agencies to combine their resources to implement the plan. A dozen communities have organized comprehensive centers, and an evaluation is under way to determine how well they work.

In West Virginia, the Governor's Cabinet on Children and Families was created in 1990 to enhance the ability of families to "protect, nurture, educate, and support the development of their children." Chaired by the governor, the cabinet includes directors of relevant executive agencies, state legislators, and representatives from higher education. Its mission is to "reinvent government" by changing the current service delivery system from "deficit models to ones that promote health, development, and well-being within the family," and by shifting from "crisis oriented services to those that focus on prevention and early intervention." The cabinet forges partnerships among citizens, community organizations, business, labor groups, local and state government bodies, advocacy groups, and members of the religious, education, and legal communities.

The primary vehicle used by the cabinet to reform services and supports for young families is the local family resource network. Operating with the support of a broadly representative leadership group, these networks serve thirty-four of West Virginia's fifty-five counties. They direct the planning and implementation of an improved system of services and supports geared to the specific needs of local children and families.

While the cabinet coordinates day-to-day improvements in children and family services, the Governor's Early Childhood Implementation Commission is developing a long-term plan to ensure the availability of high-quality early childhood services to all children, from before birth through age five. These services include health and nutrition, family support, and early childhood development and education. Working with professional groups, child advocates, business leaders, and the media, the commission is also charged with rallying broad public and professional support for the plan through periodic reports.

As it examined barriers to change, the task force noted a strong convergence of interest between those seeking to focus our nation's attention on the needs of young children and their families and those seeking to make government work more effectively on a broader scale. Current efforts to "reinvent government," through such federal mechanisms as the National Performance Review and the newly established Community Enterprise Board, represent opportunities to create more coherent strategies and more efficient delivery systems for human services, including those directed at families with young children.[11]

The Community Enterprise Board is potentially a very powerful mechanism for introducing new approaches, at the community level, to family-centered social policy. This national, cabinet-level board will designate up to nine broad "enterprise zones" and ninety-five "enterprise communities" that will be eligible for federal funding to support a range of initiatives: housing, job training, economic development, and social services, as well as technical assistance, a variety of tax incentives, and matching grants to leverage state and local resources. The goal is to enable community leaders to solve local problems with fewer bureaucratic obstacles, greater flexibility, and more emphasis on results.

The task force recommends that the Community Enterprise Board focus its investments in communities that are engaged in reforming

program strategies related to both economic development and human development. For example, the board's expenditures on employment, economic development, and housing programs in distressed communities can be effectively leveraged by similar investments in social, health, and education services that will strengthen families with young children.

Mobilize State Government

States play a critical role by establishing a framework for community action. They provide support for key services such as child care, health care, family life education, and staff training. States also play a vital role in establishing program regulations, collecting data, and allocating funds.

The task force recommends that governors and state legislatures establish mechanisms, such as those in Colorado, New Mexico, West Virginia, and several other states, to implement comprehensive program plans (including coordinated financing, staff training, and data collection) that focus on the period before conception, the prenatal period, and the first three years of life. Many states already have initiatives that focus on school readiness, but few take a comprehensive approach to promoting responsible parenthood, developing quality child care choices, ensuring good health and protection, and mobilizing communities to support families and their young children.

STATES PLAY A CRITICAL ROLE BY ESTABLISHING A FRAMEWORK FOR COMMUNITY ACTIONS.

GETTING DOWN TO WORK

The changes in community planning and government initiatives envisioned by the task force will take time. Our hope rests with the spirit and commitment that the American people demonstrate whenever a crisis threatens to block our path toward an important goal. We size up the problem, mobilize our citizenry, and get to work. In Part III of this report, the task force offers recommendations and a detailed action plan through which all sectors of society can work together to support families with young children.

PART III:

A NEW VISION: RECOMMENDATIONS
FOR ACTION

- FOR A BABY, THOSE EARLY WEEKS AND
- MONTHS OF GROWTH, UNDERSTANDING
- AND REASONING CAN NEVER BE
- BROUGHT BACK TO DO OVER AGAIN.
- THIS IS NOT THE REHEARSAL—THIS IS
- THE MAIN SHOW.
- — IRVING HARRIS

A New Vision: Recommendations for Action

The quiet crisis of families with children under three requires immediate and far-reaching action. Persuaded that strong families and communities are essential to the healthy development of our youngest children, the task force calls for a broad, integrated approach to ensure that by age three all children have had the opportunity to reach their full potential and are ready for further learning.

The problems facing our youngest children and their families cannot be solved through piecemeal action. With the support of vital institutions, both public and private, America can develop a coherent family-centered strategy to reverse the quiet crisis. Such a strategy must not be limited to governmental programs or business initiatives. All Americans must work together. If we do, we as a nation can realize our common values: strong families and communities, an informed citizenry, a productive workforce, and a competitive and strong economy. Investing in these first three years is fundamentally necessary for children themselves, for their families, and for our nation. It is time to sound—and answer—the alarm about the neglect of our nation's youngest children and their families.

The Carnegie Task Force on Meeting the Needs of Young Children calls for action in four key areas. These areas constitute vital starting points for both children and their families:

- Promote responsible parenthood
- Guarantee quality child care choices
- Ensure good health and protection
- Mobilize communities to support young children and their families

PROMOTE RESPONSIBLE PARENTHOOD

One of the most effective ways to promote healthy child development is to encourage women and men to plan and have children under positive circumstances that minimize risk for the child. Our nation must foster both personal and societal responsibility for having children. Enabling women and men to plan and act responsibly requires a national commitment to make comprehensive health services available and accessible, to educate the public about the responsibilities of raising young children, and to support the efforts of parents to carry out these responsibilities.

In order to promote responsible parenthood, the task force recommends that

- All couples, when considering the possibility of having children, should assess their age, health, and resources to ensure that they avoid unnecessary risks and can provide a healthy environment for raising a child. All parents-to-be should visit a health professional before planning to have a baby; this visit should cover the risks of smoking, drinking, and other chemical intakes; the importance of good nutrition and regular exercise; and referrals for existing problems.
- Adolescents, in particular, should avoid unnecessary risks by delaying pregnancy. To do so, adolescents need to have other age-appropriate life options.
- The full range of health-related services, including comprehensive family planning, prenatal, and postpartum health care services, should be improved, expanded, and adequately financed so that services are universally available to women as part of a minimum benefits package in health care reform.

- Families themselves should be the first source of education about parenthood, but schools, places of worship, and community-based organizations may also play a part. Education about parenting should begin in the elementary school years, but no later than early adolescence. Such education should cover, in an age-appropriate, culturally sensitive manner, human development, models of childrearing, consequences and responsibilities of parenting, available social services and supports, and human reproduction.
- States and communities should direct funds to initiate and expand community-based parent education and support programs for families with infants and toddlers. For families with high levels of stress and economic hardship, parent education and support programs must be built into a coordinated array of services, such as health care, child care, literacy classes, and job training.

GUARANTEE QUALITY CHILD CARE CHOICES

For healthy development, infants and toddlers need a continuing relationship with a few caring people, beginning with their parents and later including other child care providers. Substantial and consistent contact with parents and other caring adults allows interactions that help the baby form trusting attachments and that provide a secure base for exploring and learning about the physical and social world. This basic trust is necessary for healthy development throughout life. Infants and toddlers should develop these relationships in safe and predictable settings—in their homes or quality child care settings. Quality child care means an environment that is safe and comfortable, where children are cared for in small groups by adult caregivers, each of whom is responsible for only a few children; caregivers should be trained to meet the developmental needs of children under three years of age.

In order to guarantee good child care choices that allow parents to balance their child-rearing and workplace responsibilities, the task force recommends that

- The Family and Medical Leave Act of 1993 be strengthened by expanding coverage of parental leave to include employers with fewer than fifty employees, extending the twelve-week leave to four to six months, and providing partial wage replacement.

- The business community and all employers should consider adopting family-friendly policies such as flexible work schedules, job sharing, child care resource and referral assistance, on-site or nearby child care, and child care for sick children.

- The federal government should channel substantial new money into quality, affordable child care for families with children under three. To ensure quality, funding should be modeled on the 1990 Head Start reauthorization, mandating 25 percent of new funds for quality enhancements such as improved training, better facilities, and staff compensation. To ensure affordability, two strategies should be pursued: Federal funds should go to child care programs, permitting them to expand facilities and adopt sliding fee schedules; and the Dependent Care Tax Credit (DCTC) should be refundable for low- and moderate-income parents.

- The federal government should provide financial incentives to states to adopt standards of quality for child care, to establish timetables for the enactment of these standards, and to monitor progress toward their enforcement.

- State governments should develop and implement consistent standards of quality for child care for infants and toddlers. These standards should ensure that the environment is safe and comfortable, that children receive care in small groups, that each adult caregiver is responsible for only a few children, and that caregivers are trained to meet the developmental needs of children under three years of age.

- Every community should develop a network linking all child care programs and offering parents a variety of child care settings, including homes, centers, and Head Start programs. Communities should encourage relatives and family child care providers to participate in these networks.

- Federal and state funds should be used to promote expanded training opportunities for child care providers, including specific content on the care and development of children under age three. All providers who work with young children should have adequate training.

- Salary and benefits should be improved for child care providers. Two methods are available to link compensation with quality child care: tie higher salaries and better benefits to the completion of specialized training; and provide incentive or salary enhancement grants to child care centers and family child care networks.

ENSURE GOOD HEALTH AND PROTECTION

When young children are healthy, they are more likely to succeed in school and in time form a more productive workforce and become better parents. Few social programs offer greater long-term benefits for American society than guaranteeing good health care for all infants and toddlers: fewer children suffer from preventable illnesses and disabilities, and fewer parents bear the burden of caring for sick children and paying their medical bills. The health care needs of infants and toddlers call for services that are broader in scope and that, in certain instances, are of greater intensity and duration than those designed for older children and adults. Good health, of course, involves more than medical care. Being healthy also means being safe. Infants and toddlers need to grow up in homes where they are emotionally and physically safe from injury and harm. Young children must live in neighborhoods in which their families are confident they can protect and safely raise them.

In order to ensure good health and protection, the task force recommends that

- Comprehensive health care services should be available to all pregnant women, infants, and toddlers as part of a minimum benefits package in health care reform. These services must include primary and preventive care, including immunizations. Pregnant women, infants, and toddlers should be the first to be included in a universal system of health care.

- Home visiting services by trained professionals should be made available to all first-time mothers during the first six weeks of the child's life. These visits should provide important health services, parenting infor-

mation, and referral to community resources. In addition, more comprehensive home visiting services should be available from the prenatal period through the first three years of life to families who are at risk for poor maternal and child health outcomes.

- The Women, Infants and Children (WIC) nutritional supplementation program should be expanded to ensure that it reaches all eligible pregnant and nursing women, infants, and children.

- New public strategies should be developed to reduce the incidence of unintentional injuries in infants and toddlers. The prevention of injuries should be made a national priority through broad-based community efforts to educate parents and other adults.

- National, state, and local laws must stringently control possession of firearms. Parents and other adults must be informed about the dangers to young children of having a gun in the house and must store weapons safely if they have them. However, many parents will accept or act on this only when they are confident that their communities are safe.

- To reduce child abuse and neglect, proven parent education, support, and counseling programs should be expanded to teach parents skills in nonviolent conflict resolution. Community-based programs should be developed to train professionals to help families and children cope with the effects of living in unsafe and violent communities.

Mobilize Communities to Support Young Children and Their Families

There is a growing recognition that comprehensive community supports and services are necessary to ensure the healthy development of our youngest children. Unfortunately, community services for families with children under three are few and fragmentary. And families of all kinds are finding they need more help in balancing childrearing and workplace responsibilities, gaining access to the best possible child care and health care, and dealing with the stresses of raising a young family. This is the quiet crisis that threatens the stability of community and family life across the nation.

To reverse this crisis, the old ways of providing services and supports must be reassessed, and new approaches must be found to ensure that every family with a newborn is linked to a source of health care, child care, and parenting support. To mobilize communities, the task force recommends that

- Every community in America should focus attention on children under three and their families, beginning in the period before conception. Community leadership groups should develop a strategic plan that includes a needs assessment and clear goals; an action plan to strengthen and link programs, monitor quality, and measure performance; and an analysis of how resources can be reallocated and expanded.

- Broad experimentation with creating family-centered communities should be undertaken. Two approaches appear especially promising:

  - Create neighborhood family and child centers to provide and enhance services and supports for all families. These centers should provide parenting supports

and education; offer other needed services and access to information about community resources, including comprehensive health services and quality child care; provide professional development for staff working with families with young children; and strengthen collaboration among the business community, advocacy groups, the media, and programs that deliver services and supports to children and families.

- Expand and adapt the Head Start model to meet the needs of low-income families with infants and toddlers. Beginning with the most disadvantaged families, the new programs for younger children should include home visits, immunizations, other health and prenatal care, parent support, and developmentally sound child care, as well as nutritional and social services. They would also equip parents to be the effective first teachers of their young children and could link up with adult job training, drug treatment, and economic development programs. Head Start programs for younger children could be attached to schools, settlement houses, existing Head Start programs, or other community institutions.

- The President should direct a high-level federal group to coordinate federal agency support on behalf of young children and families. This group should assess and take action to remove the specific obstacles that states and communities face in providing more effective services and supports to families with children under age three.

- The Community Enterprise Board, which funds community and economic development programs, should also fund programs to strengthen families with infants and toddlers.

- Governors and state legislatures should establish mechanisms to adopt and implement comprehensive policy and program plans that focus on the prenatal period and children under age three.

A CALL TO ACTION

Parents and experts have long known that the first three years of life are crucial to a child's well-being and ability to learn. In recent years, research has borne out these observations, showing that the quality and variety of early experiences have a decisive, sustained impact on a child's healthy development. We can now say with greater confidence than ever before that investments in the first three years of life will produce lasting benefits for the children themselves, for their families, for our communities, and for our nation.

The task force calls upon all sectors of American society to join together to offer a decent start in life to all children under the age of three.

- We ask the *President* to direct a high-level federal group to review the findings of this report, and to ensure the adequacy, coherence, and coordination of federal programs for families with young children. We urge him to introduce legislation to expand Head Start to serve children under three, to strengthen the Family and Medical Leave Act, to include pregnant women and young children in health care reform, and to channel new money into quality child care for families with children under three.

- In the spirit of "reinventing government," we urge *federal agencies* to identify and remove the obstacles that states and communities encounter as they implement federally funded programs or test innovative solutions.

- We call upon *Congress* to enact legislation that focuses resources more sharply on the needs of children under age three and their families. We urge Congress to enact legislation that strengthens the Family and Medical Leave Act and that provides increased resources for quality child care and parent education and support. Congress should ensure that pregnant women and all children under three are the first to be included in health care reform.

- We call upon *states* to convene or form child and family councils to review this report and consider its implications for children under age three in each state and its communities. We urge every state to review its legislative and regulatory framework, particularly standards in child care, with a view toward raising the quality of existing services and creating incentives for local innovation.

- We call upon *community leaders* to assess the adequacy of existing services for families with young children (especially those with multiple risks), to recommend specific steps to improve and coordinate services, and to introduce mechanisms for monitoring results. We ask them to create or strengthen existing neighborhood family and child centers in order to meet the needs of families with young children.

- We call upon the *private and philanthropic sectors,* including foundations, to pay more attention to families with children under three, and to expand their support of initiatives that give our youngest children a decent start in life. We urge community foundations to support local efforts to direct attention and resources to meet the needs of young children.

- We urge *educators,* working with other community agencies, to incorporate services to children under age three in their plans for the schools of the twenty-first century. We urge a substantial expansion of efforts to educate young people about parenthood. We ask educators in secondary schools and community colleges to provide more training and technical assistance to child care providers.

- We call upon *health care decision makers* to include, in any plan for national health care reform, family planning services, comprehensive prenatal care for expectant mothers and universal primary and preventive care for young children. We ask them to give serious consideration to a specific standard of coverage and service for young children.

- We urge *service providers* in child care, health, and social services to take a family-centered approach to meeting the needs of young children and the adults who care for them. We ask them to offer staff, parents, and other caregivers opportunities to learn more about the needs of families with young children, about child development, and about promoting children's health and safety.

- We call upon *business leaders* to support policies that result in family-friendly workplaces, in particular strengthening the Family and Medical Leave Act of 1993, introducing flexible work schedules, and providing assistance with child care. We ask corporate leaders who are on the cutting edge of these policy innovations to help businesses of every size to adopt family-friendly policies.

- We call upon the *media* to deliver strong messages about responsible motherhood and fatherhood and to portray family life in ways that further parents' understanding of the importance of the first three years and give all of us insight into the quiet crisis. We urge them to publicize information about preventing injuries—the leading cause of death and disability of children under age four.

- Perhaps most important, we call upon *mothers and fathers* to do everything in their power to secure the knowledge and resources they need to plan and raise children responsibly. When these resources are not available, we urge them to make their needs known to government representatives, community leaders, and service providers.

All Americans must work together, in their homes, workplaces, and communities, to ensure that children under the age of three—our most vulnerable citizens—are given the care and protection they need and deserve. Nothing less than the well-being of our society and its vital institutions is at stake.

OF COURSE WE NEED CHILDREN!
ADULTS NEED CHILDREN IN THEIR LIVES
TO LISTEN TO AND CARE FOR, TO KEEP
THEIR IMAGINATION FRESH AND THEIR
HEARTS YOUNG AND TO MAKE THE
FUTURE A REALITY FOR WHICH THEY
ARE WILLING TO WORK.
— MARGARET MEAD

APPENDIXES

Appendix A

CONSULTANTS TO THE TASK FORCE

Jeanne Barr
Research Assistant
The Stanford Center for the Study of Families,
    Children and Youth
Stanford University
Stanford, California

Terry Bond
Vice President
Families and Work Institute
New York, New York

Sarah S. Brown
Senior Study Director
Board on Children and Their Families
Institute of Medicine, National Academy
    of Sciences
Washington, DC

Sanford M. Dornbusch
Chair of Advisory Board
The Stanford Center for the Study of Families,
    Children and Youth
Stanford University
Stanford, California

Ellen Galinsky
Co-President
Families and Work Institute
New York, New York

Naomi Goldstein
Executive Officer for the Assistant Secretary of
    Planning and Evaluation
United States Department of Health and Human
    Services
Washington, DC

Sheila B. Kamerman
Professor and Co-Director
Cross National Studies
Columbia University School of Social Work
Columbia University
New York, New York

Joan Lombardi
Policy Consultant
Administration for Children and Families
United States Department of Health and
    Human Services
Washington, DC

Judith S. Musick
Vice Chairman
The Ounce of Prevention
Chicago, Illinois

Joy D. Osofsky
Professor of Pediatrics and Psychiatry
Louisiana State University Medical Center
New Orleans, Louisiana

Mark J. Schlesinger
Professor
Yale Medical School
New Haven, Connecticut, and
Rutgers University
New Brunswick, New Jersey

Victoria Poole
Assistant Professor of Nursing
University of Alabama at Birmingham
Birmingham, Alabama

Nathalie Vanderpool
Consultant in Health/Education Policy
Philadelphia, Pennsylvania

Appendix B

PAPERS COMMISSIONED BY THE TASK FORCE ON MEETING THE NEEDS OF YOUNG CHILDREN

Peggy Pizzo, "Financing Family Centered Infant Care," June 1992.

Sarah S. Brown, "Health Care Benefits for Children: Their Content and Cost," January 1993.

Ellen Galinsky and Terry Bond, "Parental Leave for American Workers," January 1993.

Naomi Goldstein, "Are Changes in Work and Family Harming Children?" January 1993.

Joan Lombardi, "Expanding and Enhancing Head Start Services to Younger Children," January 1993.

Edward Zigler, "An Earlier Head Start: Planning an Intervention Program for Economically Disadvantaged Families and Children Ages Zero to Three," January 1993.

Naomi Goldstein, "Services That Work: A Report," February 1993.

Lorraine V. Klerman, "Young Children in the United States: Are We Meeting Their Needs?" February 1993.

Lorraine V. Klerman, Sarah S. Brown, and Victoria L. Poole, "The Role of Family Planning in Promoting Healthy Child Development," February 1993.

Mark Schlesinger, "The Interaction of Poverty and Service Interventions of Young Children," February 1993.

Sheila B. Kamerman, "Meeting the Needs of Very Young Children and Their Families: The Importance of a Dual Strategy," May 1993.

Nathalie Vanderpool, "Young Children and Families: Creating a Social Policy Agenda; A Review of Selected Reports," May 1993.

Sanford Dornbusch, Jeanne A. Barr, and Natalie A. Seer, "The Impact of Education for Parenting Upon Parents, Children and Family Systems," June 1993.

Joy Osofsky, "Violence in the Lives of Young Children," June 1993.

Judith Musick, "Carnegie Primer on the First Three Years of Life," September 1993.

Appendix C

INVITEES, "SERVICES THAT WORK" MEETING, JANUARY 27–28, 1993*

C. Robin Britt, Sr.
Secretary of Human Resources
State of North Carolina
Raleigh, North Carolina

Sarah S. Brown
Senior Study Director
Institute of Medicine
Washington, DC

Barbara Clinton
Director
Center for Health Services
Vanderbilt University Medical Center
Nashville, Tennessee

Evelyn Davis
Assistant Clinical Professor of Pediatrics
Harlem Hospital
New York, New York

Ana O. Dumois
Executive Director
Community Family Planning Council
New York, New York

Karen Edwards
Executive Director
Select Committee on Children and Youth
Nashville, Tennessee

Frank Farrow
Director
Children's Services Policy
Washington, DC

Caroline Gaston
Administrative Assistant to the First Lady
Governor's Office
Santa Fe, New Mexico

Olivia A. Golden
Director of Programs and Policy
Children's Defense Fund
Washington, DC

* Affiliations as of January 1993.

Naomi Goldstein
Center for Perinatal Health
Brigham and Women's Hospital
Boston, Massachusetts

Elizabeth H. Graham
Assistant Commissioner
Bureau of Maternal Services and Family Planning
Department of Health
New York, New York

Neal Halfon
Associate Professor
School of Public Health
University of California, Los Angeles
Los Angeles, California

Max M. Heller
Former Mayor
Greenville, South Carolina

Judith Jerald
Project Director
Windham County Family Support Program
Brattleboro, Vermont

Judith E. Jones
Director
National Center for Children in Poverty
School of Public Health
Columbia University
New York, New York

Sheila B. Kamerman
Professor and Co-Director
Cross National Studies
Columbia University School of Social Work
New York, New York

Harriet Kitzman
New Mothers Study
Pediatrics Department
University of Rochester Medical Center
Rochester, New York

Marion S. Levine
Executive Director
North Shore Family and Child Guidance Center
Roslyn Heights, New York

Joan Lombardi
Alexandria, Virginia

James R. McCabe
Superintendent
Lake County School District R-1
Leadville, Colorado

Janice Molnar
Program Officer for Urban Poverty
Ford Foundation
New York, New York

Mary Ellen O'Keeffe
Executive Director
Children's Trust Foundation
Seattle, Washington

Deborah Phillips
Associate Professor of Psychology
University of Virginia
Charlottesville, Virginia

Julius B. Richmond
John D. MacArthur Professor of Health
    Policy Emeritus
Department of Social Medicine
Harvard Medical School
Boston, Massachusetts

Gloria G. Rodriguez
National President
Avance Family Support and Education Program
San Antonio, Texas

Jo-Anna L. Rorie
Faculty
Nurse-Midwifery Education Program
Boston University School of Public Health
Boston, Massachusetts

Kenneth J. Ryan
Chairman
Department of Obstetrics and Gynecology
Brigham and Women's Hospital
Boston, Massachusetts

Jean Sabharwal
Director
The Family Care Center
Lexington, Kentucky

Aaron Shirley
Project Director
Jackson–Hinds Community Health Center
Jackson, Mississippi

Sarah Cardwell Shuptrine
President
Sarah Shuptrine and Associates
Columbia, South Carolina

Patti Siegel
California Child Care Resource and Referral Network
San Francisco, California

Justine Strickland
Educational Consultant
Stone Mountain, Georgia

Eleanor S. Szanton
Executive Director
Zero to Three—National Center for Clinical
    Infant Programs
Arlington, Virginia

Bernice Weissbourd
Family Focus, Inc.
Chicago, Illinois

Mildred M. Winter
Executive Director
Parents as Teachers National Center Inc.
St. Louis, Missouri

Wendy C. Wolf
President
Center for Assessment and Policy Development
Bala Cynwyd, Pennsylvania

Barry Zuckerman
Office of the President
Brigham and Women's Hospital
Boston, Massachusetts

Appendix D

BIOGRAPHIES OF TASK FORCE MEMBERS AND STAFF

Richard W. Riley chaired the task force until February 1993, when he was nominated by President Clinton as secretary of education. From 1978 to 1987 he was governor of South Carolina, and he has provided national and state leadership in both education and health reform. Governor Riley was a member of the National Commission to Prevent Infant Mortality and chaired both the Southern Corporate Coalition to Improve Maternal and Child Health and the Southern Regional Education Board Commission for Educational Quality. Governor Riley has received numerous awards, including the Government Responsibility Award from the Martin Luther King, Jr., Center and the Harold W. McGraw Jr. Prize in Education.

Eleanor E. Maccoby has co-chaired the task force since February 1993. A member of the faculty of the psychology department of Stanford University since 1958, Professor Maccoby received her Ph.D. from the University of Michigan in 1950. Her primary field of interest has been the development of children's social behavior, particularly as it relates to family functioning and parental child-rearing methods. She has written many books and articles, most recently *Dividing the Child: The Social and Legal Dilemmas of Custody* (Maccoby and Mnookin, November 1992); a book on the adjustment of adolescents in divorced families is in preparation. The recipient of many honors and awards, Dr. Maccoby has been a member of the Institute of Medicine since 1977; she was elected to the National Academy of Sciences in 1993.

Julius B. Richmond, who has co-chaired the task force since February 1993, is John D. MacArthur Professor of Health Policy Emeritus at Harvard University. He chaired the steering committee of the Forum on the Future of Children and Families of the National Academy of Sciences. Dr. Richmond is a former surgeon general and former assistant secretary of the Department of Health and Human Services. He was also the first director of the national Head Start program. Dr. Richmond has received many honors and awards.

Diane Asselin is the producer of "Growing up Together," a Lifetime Television series designed to help viewers with the challenging job of raising children from pregnancy through the first five years of life. An Emmy Award–winning producer, she has developed and pro-

duced eleven network specials for family viewing on such subjects as the adolescence of a deaf teenager and the testing for drugs in high school. Her most recent project is a PBS prime-time special funded by the National Science Foundation, Arco, and the Norris Foundation: "Count on Me" combines comedy, drama, music, and real-life vignettes to encourage parents to participate in their child's education, at school and at home, with the emphasis on math.

Kathryn E. Barnard is a professor of nursing and adjunct professor of psychology at the University of Washington, where she has also served as associate dean of the School of Nursing. For the past 30 years, she has been a scholar, researcher, and educator with interests in children and parenting. She coordinated the risk and prevention group for the John D. and Catherine T. MacArthur Foundation's health network on the transition to early childhood. Her research has focused on the interaction of children with their environment, particularly infants at biological and environmental risk. She is president of Zero to Three—the National Center for Clinical Infant Programs. She is a member of the American Academy of Nursing and the Institute of Medicine and has received many awards in nursing and public health.

Owen Bradford Butler is chairman of the board of directors of Northern Telecom Ltd.; he was formerly chairman of the board of directors of the Procter and Gamble Company. Mr. Butler was chair of a subcommittee of the Committee for Economic Development (CED) that produced a policy statement in 1985 on business and the public schools entitled "Investing In Our Children." In 1987 another subcommittee of the CED issued a policy statement entitled "Children in Need — Investment Strategies for the Educationally Disadvantaged"; Mr. Butler chaired this subcommittee as well. A graduate of Dartmouth College, he is a director of many companies, including Deere & Co., Armco Inc., and Berlitz International. He is the immediate past chairman of the board of trustees of the CED and has encouraged the business community to contribute to the knowledge, development, and skills of America's children.

Ramon C. Cortines has been chancellor of the New York City Board of Education since September 1993. He left the task force in April 1993, when he began work with the Clinton administration; he later became Assistant Secretary for Intergovernmental and Interagency Affairs in the United States Department of Education. In an education career of more than 30 years, Mr. Cortines has taught and held administrative positions at virtually all levels in the school systems in which he served. He was superintendent of schools of the Pasadena (California) Unified School District from 1972 to 1978 and again from 1979 to 1984 and was superintendent of the San Jose Unified School district from 1984 to 1986; he headed the San Francisco Unified School district from 1986 to 1992. Before joining the Clinton administration, Mr. Cortines had been consultant professor at Stanford University and associate director of the Pew Charitable Trusts Forum on School Reform.

Ezra C. Davidson, Jr., is professor and chairman of the department of obstetrics and gynecology at Charles R. Drew University of Medicine and Science, a position he has held since 1971. He also holds professorships in obstetrics and gynecology at UCLA and Dartmouth Schools of Medicine and is chief-of-service, Department of Obstetrics and Gynecology, at the King–Drew Medical Center in Los Angeles. A graduate of Meharry Medical College, Dr. Davidson has been active in research, education, and clinical and public services. He was an early contributor to the development of the technology of fetoscopy and fetal blood sampling. He was a Robert Wood Johnson Health Policy Fellow at the Institute of Medicine in 1979–1980, during which time he served as a health advisor to Senator Bill Bradley of New Jersey. A former president of the American College of Obstetricians and Gynecologists, he has lectured widely, both domestically and internationally, and has received many honors and awards.

John D. Deardourff is a cofounder of Bailey, Deardourff & Associates, one of the leading political planning, consulting, and advertising firms in the United States. Mr. Deardourff has lectured widely on government and politics, and he has been a guest on various public affairs television programs. He is a consultant to Planned Parenthood and has received the National Women's Political Caucus's annual "Good Guy" Award. He is a director of the Women's Campaign Research Fund and a trustee of the Children's Defense Fund and of Public Voice, a consumer advocacy organization concerned with national food and health policy. He is a member of the development committee of the Black Student Fund and a director of The American Political Network. Mr. Deardourff received his M.A. from the Fletcher School of Law and Diplomacy and was a fellow of the Institute of Politics at Harvard University and a Conroy Fellow at St. Paul's School, Concord, New Hampshire.

Irving B. Harris is chairman of the executive committee and director of the Pittway Corporation; he is also chairman of both the Pittway Corporation Charitable Foundation and the Harris Foundation. A graduate of Yale University, Mr. Harris has spent more than 40 years as a business leader committed to furthering the interests of children and families. As a member of the National Commission on Children and the Committee for Economic Development, he brought the business perspective to the nation's deliberations on the human service needs and strengths of families. Currently chairman emeritus of Family Focus, Inc., and the Erickson Institute and cofounder and chairman of the Ounce of Prevention Fund, he has received numerous awards and honors.

John W. Hatch is a professor in the health behavior and health education department at the University of North Carolina School of Public Health. He received his M.S.W. from Atlanta University and his Dr.P.H. from the University of North Carolina. For the past twenty-one years, Dr. Hatch has been involved in teaching and research related to health and development. His area of expertise is in health promotion and disease prevention with Black church organizations as sponsor organizations. Dr. Hatch is the immediate past moderator of the Medical Commission of the World Council of Churches, Geneva, Switzerland. He is a board member of Freedom From Hunger Foundation, Physicians For Human Rights, and the Baptist Foundation.

Fred M. Hechinger, senior advisor at Carnegie Corporation of New York, has devoted much of his career as a reporter, columnist, editor, author, and foundation executive to issues of education and policies affecting children and society. Mr. Hechinger started his journalistic career in 1947 as a foreign correspondent for the Overseas News

Agency and the Bridgeport *Sunday Herald*. He later served as an education columnist for the *Washington Post* and was American correspondent for the Education Supplement of the *Times* of London and education editor of *Parents* magazine. In 1959, Mr. Hechinger joined the *New York Times* as education editor. He later served on that newspaper's editorial board, becoming deputy editor of the editorial page. In 1978, he became president of The New York Times Company Foundation and of The New York Times Neediest Cases Fund and began writing a weekly column, "About Education." He left the *Times* in 1990. Mr. Hechinger is the author of several books on education. He has received numerous awards, including the British Empire Medal and the City College Distinguished Alumni Medal.

Max M. Heller founded Maxon Shirt Company in 1948; he retired from the firm in 1969 to devote his time to public affairs, with particular emphasis on improving neighborhoods and human relations through a combination of business expertise and community activism. In 1969, he was elected to the Greenville, South Carolina, City Council. In 1971, he was elected mayor of Greenville for a four-year term; he was reelected in 1975. In January 1979, he was appointed by Governor Riley as chairman of the State Development Board, a position that he held until July 1983. He is a past president of the Greenville Housing Foundation and has served on many state and national boards. In 1988 he received the Urban League's "Whitney Young" Humanitarian Award.

Shirley Mount Hufstedler is a partner is the law firm of Hufstedler, Kaus & Ettinger. She received her Bachelor of Business Administration degree from the University of New Mexico and her Bachelor of Law degree from Stanford University. Having served as special legal consultant to the Attorney General of California in the complex Colorado River litigation before the United States Supreme Court in 1960–1961, she was appointed judge of the Los Angeles County Supreme Court in 1961, and in 1966 she was appointed associate justice of the California Court of Appeals. In September 1968, President Johnson appointed her Judge of the United States Court of Appeals for the Ninth Circuit, where she served for eleven years until she became President Carter's secretary of education. Since 1981, Mrs. Hufstedler has been teaching and practicing law; she also serves on several corporate boards. Mrs. Hufstedler has written numerous articles on the law, education, government, and national and international affairs and has received many honorary degrees and awards.

A. Sidney Johnson III is executive director of the American Public Welfare Association, which represents all fifty state human service agencies, 800 local departments, and 4,000 individuals. Mr. Johnson was special assistant to the late HEW Secretary Wilbur Cohen and was legislative aide to Senator Walter F. Mondale; he spent five years as staff director of the Senate Subcommittee on Children and Youth. In 1976 he founded the Family Impact Seminar in Washington, the nation's first organization devoted to examining the impact of public and private policies on American families. From 1982 to 1985 he was executive director of the American Association for Marriage and Family Therapy. In 1988 he was named by the Speaker of the House of Representatives to serve on the National Commission on Children to review national policies affecting children. Mr. Johnson received his M.S.W. from the University of Michigan and his B.A. from Williams College.

Judith E. Jones is director of the National Center for Children in Poverty (NCCP) and associate clinical professor of Public Health at Columbia University. Professor Jones also directs the national program office of the Robert Wood Johnson Foundation's new five-year initiative "Free to Grow: Head Start Partnerships to Promote Substance-free Communities." She had earlier served as deputy director, Center for Population and Family Health, Columbia University, where she designed and managed the implementation of comprehensive school-based clinics at the middle-school level, as well as a widely acclaimed intervention to streamline Medicaid certification to increase early prenatal care. Professor Jones received her B.A. degree in psychology from Hunter College and her M.S. degree in business policy from Columbia University. Professor Jones has recently been appointed by the secretary of health and human services to the Advisory Committee on Head Start Quality and Expansion. She has served on many national boards and commissions.

Thomas H. Kean is president of Drew University, chairman of the New American Schools Development Corporation, and chairman of the National Environmental Education and Training Foundation. Governor of New Jersey from 1987 to 1990, he was a close advisor to President Bush on education, the environment, housing, volunteerism, and other national policy issues. As governor, Kean, a former history teacher, initiated nearly forty reforms in the state's public education system. Governor Kean is the chairman of Educate America and serves on the board of the National Association of Independent College and Universities, Carnegie Corporation of New

York, and Campus Compact. He holds a B.A. from Princeton University and an M.A. from Columbia University Teachers College, where he is a trustee, and has received many honorary degrees.

Lorraine V. Klerman is professor and chair, Department of Maternal and Child Health, the University of Alabama at Birmingham. Professor Klerman also has appointments in the university's Department of Pediatrics and Civitan International Research Center. She received her master's and doctoral degrees in public health from Harvard University. Professor Klerman has studied and written extensively about the federal maternal and child health program, adolescent childbearing, services for pregnant women, school absence, and the relationship between poverty and child health. She has served on several national, state, and local advisory boards; federal study sections; and journal editorial boards. Professor Klerman works closely with county and state governments in the South on programs related to maternal and child health.

Ray Marshall, who was secretary of labor under President Carter, holds the Audre and Bernard Rapoport Centennial Chair in Economics and Public Affairs at the University of Texas—Austin. He holds a Ph.D. in Economics from the University of California—Berkeley, and is the author or co-author of more than 200 books, monographs, and articles on such topics as the economics of the family; education and the economy; U.S. competitiveness in an internationalized economy; labor in the South; international workers' rights; and minority business development. His most recent book, *Thinking for a Living: Education and the Wealth of Nations* (with Marc Tucker), was published in 1992 by Basic Books.

Vonnie C. McLoyd is a professor of psychology at the University of Michigan and a research scientist at the university's Center for Human Growth and Development. She received her Ph.D. from the University of Michigan in 1975. She has served on the Science Policy Working Group of the Carnegie Council on Adolescent Development, chaired and served on review panels for the Program Committees of Society for Research in Child Development (SRCD) and the American Psychological Association, and chaired the Black Caucus of SRCD. She is a member of the governing council of the SRCD and of the editorial boards of several journals. Dr. McLoyd was a William T. Grant Faculty Scholar in Child Mental Health from 1986 to 1991. Her recent research tests models of the mechanisms by which economic hardship affects emotional and social development in African American adolescents.

Deborah Phillips is director of the Board on Children and Families of the National Research Council's Commission on Behavioral and Social Sciences and Education and the Institute of Medicine. She is on leave as associate professor of psychology at the University of Virginia. Dr. Phillips received her Ph.D. in developmental psychology at Yale University. She was the first director of the Child Care Information Service of the National Association for the Education of Young Children and is a member of many task forces and advisory groups that address child and family policy issues, including the research task force of the Secretary's Advisory Committee on Head Start Quality and Expansion of the U.S. Department of Health and Human Services. Dr. Phillips has testified frequently before Congress on issues of child care quality.

Gloria G. Rodriguez is founder and national president of the Avance Family Support and Education Program. Dr. Rodriguez earned her Ph.D. in early childhood education from the University of Texas at Austin. In 1990, she received the first "Attitude Award" presented by Lifetime's nationally syndicated program "Attitudes" for changing public attitudes toward family services. Dr. Rodriguez was a charter board member of the National Family Resource Coalition (1982–1989), and has acted as a consultant to the federal government, the Harvard Family Research Project, Georgetown University, and the Bush Center at Yale. She served on the Texas Health and Human Services Coordinating Council and was appointed to Governor Ann Richards' transition team in early childhood education; she currently chairs the Governor's Head Start state collaboration task force.

Kenneth J. Ryan, a graduate of Harvard Medical School, has spent more than 25 years in teaching, research, writing, and practice devoted to improving the reproductive health of women. He is chairman of the department of obstetrics and gynecology at Brigham and Women's Hospital in Boston. In the late 1960s he served on the President's Committee on Mental Retardation, and in the 1970s he was chairman of the National Commission for the Protection of Human Subjects of Biomedical and Behavioral Research. He has had a longstanding interest in ethical issues in medicine and reproductive health. Dr. Ryan has received numerous awards and honors, including the Weinstein Award of United Cerebral Palsy and the President's Award of the Society of Gynecological Investigation; he has also held office in several professional organizations.

Jonas Salk received his M.D. degree from New York University College of Medicine. The polio vaccine that bears his name was licensed for public use on April 12, 1955. In the early 1960s, Dr. Salk founded the Salk Institute for Biological Studies, bringing together scientists and scholars from different disciplines who shared a common interest in science and in the human implications of their work. The institute began operation in 1963; today, with a support staff and research faculty of over 500, it is at the forefront in the advancement of knowledge of the complex biological systems. Dr. Salk has also been assisting international health agencies, as well as governmental and local health officials, in improving immunization programs in developing countries. He has written several books about the prospects and alternatives for the human future, including *The Survival of the Wise*.

Isabel V. Sawhill was a member of the Carnegie Task Force on Meeting the Needs of Young Children until her designation by President Clinton as associate director, human resources, Office of Management and Budget, in February 1993. Before her appointment, Dr. Sawhill was a senior fellow at the Urban Institute; from 1981 to 1990 she was director (or codirector) of the institute's Changing Domestic Priorities project. Dr. Sawhill's most recent book is *Challenge to Leadership: Economic and Social Issues for the Next Decade*, published in 1988. She is a trustee of the American Assembly, the Manpower Development Research Corporation, the Population Reference Bureau, and Resources for the Future. Dr. Sawhill attended Wellesley College and received both her B.A. and Ph.D. degrees in economics from New York University.

Lisbeth B. Schorr is a lecturer in social medicine at Harvard University, a member of the Harvard University Working Group on Early Life, and director of the Harvard University Project on Effective Services. Her book, *Within Our Reach: Breaking the Cycle of Disadvantage* (with Daniel Schorr) has influenced policymakers, practitioners, and advocates for more effective human services. Ms. Schorr is a member of the National Academy of Sciences' Board on Children and Families and the board of the Foundation for Child Development. In 1993, Ms. Schorr was appointed to the executive committee of the Harvard University Project on Schooling and Children. Between 1978 and 1980, Ms. Schorr chaired the congressionally mandated Select Panel for the Promotion of Child Health, and in the early 1970s she helped to establish the health division of the Children's Defense Fund.

Sarah Cardwell Shuptrine is president of Sarah Shuptrine and Associates, a health and social policy research firm based in Columbia, South Carolina. She is also founder and president of the Southern Institute on Children and Families. From 1985 to 1986, Ms. Shuptrine was executive assistant to Governor Richard W. Riley for health and human services. As chief policy advisor to the governor, Ms. Shuptrine served as director of the South Carolina Children's Coordinating Cabinet and led numerous statewide initiatives on behalf of disadvantaged citizens. From 1984 to 1985, she chaired the work group for the Southern Regional Task Force on Infant Mortality, and in 1988 Ms. Shuptrine was appointed to the National Commission on Children by the Speaker of the United States House of Representatives. In 1992, she cochaired two task forces of the Commission, one on establishing family support programs and one on coordinating services for children and families.

Michael S. Wald, now deputy general counsel, Office of the General Counsel, Department of Health and Human Services, was a member of the task force through June 1993. Professor Wald was Jackson Eli Reynolds Professor of Law at Stanford University, where he had taught since 1967. His research focused on treatment of children in the legal system, and he taught courses dealing with public policy towards children. He also drafted the American Bar Association's Standards Related to Abused and Neglected Children and helped draft the Adoption Assistance and Child Welfare Act of 1980. His publications include *The Conditions of Children in California* (1989), for which he was the general editor, and *Protecting Abused and Neglected Children* (1988) with M. Carlsmith and P. Leiderman. He has served as a juvenile court judge in California and has been a member of the board of directors of the National Committee for the Prevention of Child Abuse and of the National Research Council's Committee on Child Development Research and Public Policy.

Edward Zigler is the Sterling Professor of Psychology, head of the psychology section of the Child Study Center, and director of the Bush Center in Child Development and Social Policy. Professor Zigler received his B.A. and M.A. degrees from the University of Missouri at Kansas City and his Ph.D. in clinical psychology from the University of Texas at Austin. Professor Zigler's scholarly work addresses mental retardation, psychopathology, intervention programs for economically disadvantaged children, and the effects of out-of-home care on the children of working parents. He has published widely. He was the first director of the Office of Child Development (now the Administration for Children, Youth and Families) and was chief of the U.S. Children's Bureau. He helped plan both Project Head Start and Project Follow Through. Professor Zigler has served as a special consultant to numerous cabinet officers and private foundations, and he often testifies as an expert witness before congressional committees.

Barry Zuckerman is professor and chairman of the department of pediatrics at the Boston University School of Medicine and director of the Division of Developmental and Behavioral Pediatrics at Boston City Hospital. Dr. Zuckerman has developed model programs involving collaboration between pediatricians and educators to meet the needs of at-risk young children. He is a member of the National Commission on Children, chairman of the Section of Developmental and Behavioral Pediatrics of the American Academy of Pediatrics, and a member of many state and national organizations. Dr. Zuckerman has conducted research and written extensively on the impact of biological and environmental factors on the health and development of young children, especially those living in poverty.

STAFF

Kathryn Taaffe Young, the task force's director of studies, is the principal author of its report. Dr. Young received her doctorate in developmental psychology from Yale University in 1988. She is a visiting research scientist at the Bush Center for Child Development and Social Policy at Yale University. From 1988 to 1992 Dr. Young was a senior program officer at the Smith Richardson Foundation, where she directed the work of the Children and Families at Risk program. Before that, she was a faculty member at Sarah Lawrence College and a Fellow of the National Center for Clinical Infant Programs. As a developmental psychologist, she has focused on contextual influences in infant development. Her historical survey of the parenting literature identified the extent to which scientific knowledge and cultural ideologies about infants have been part of expert advice to parents; the study was recently published in *Child Development*. She is currently documenting the nature and role of parental beliefs in infant development.

Linda Randolph, the task force's executive director until September 30, 1993, received her M.D. degree from the Howard University College of Medicine and her M.P.H. degree in Maternal and Child Health from the University of California at Berkeley. For seven years, Dr. Randolph was national director of health services, Project Head Start. In 1980, she became the New York State Health Department's Associate Commissioner for New York City affairs, and, in 1983, she became director of the Office of Public Health, New York State Department of Health. In 1990, Dr. Randolph was appointed Professor of Health Policy and Management at the State University of New York at Albany, and in 1991 she also assumed the position of director of the Master of Public Health Program in the Graduate School of Public Health. In October 1991, Dr. Randolph was appointed Clinical Professor in the Department of Community Medicine, Mount Sinai School of Medicine.

REFERENCES

PART I: THE QUIET CRISIS

The Quiet Crisis

1. National Education Goals Panel. Building a Nation of Learners: The National Education Goals Report. Executive summary. Washington, DC, 1993.
2. H. Chugani. Positron emission tomography scanning in newborns. *Clinics in Perinatology* 20(2):398, June 1993.
3. B. Kolb. Brain development, plasticity, and behavior. *American Psychologist* 44(9):1203-1212, 1989.
4. Ibid, p. 1205.
5. Infant Health and Development Program. Enhancing the outcomes of low-birth-weight premature infants. *Journal of the American Medical Association* 263:3035–3042, 1990.
   C. Ramey *et al.*, The Infant Health Development Program for low birth weight, premature infants: program elements, family participation, and child intelligence. *Pediatrics* 89:454–465, 1992.
6. F. A. Campbell and C. T. Ramey. Mid-adolescent outcomes for high risk students: An examination of the continuing effects of early intervention. *In* Craig T. Ramey (Chair), Efficacy of early intervention for poverty children: Results of three longitudinal studies. Symposium presented at the biennial meeting of the Society for Research in Child Development, New Orleans, 1993.
7. H. Chugani, M. E. Phelps, and J. C. Mazziotta. Positron emission tomography study of human brain functional development. *Annals of Neurology* 22(4):495, 1987.
8. B. S. McEwen. Hormones and brain development. Address to the American Health Foundation, Washington, DC, April 2, 1992.
9. G. R. Patterson. Performance models for antisocial boys. *American Psychologist* 41:432–444, 1986.
   E. E. Werner and R. S. Smith. *Vulnerable but Invincible: A Longitudinal Study of Resilient Children and Youth.* New York: Adams, Bannister, Cox, 1982.

M. Rutter. Protective factors in children's responses to stress and disadvantage, pp. 49–74. *In* M. W. Kent, and J. E. Rolf (editors), *Primary Prevention of Psychopathology: Vol. 3. Social Competence in Children.* Hanover, NH: University Press of New England, 1979.
10. R. Loeber. Development and risk factors of juvenile antisocial behavior and delinquency. *Clinical Psychology Review* 10:1–41, 1990.
   K. MacDonald. Early experience, relative plasticity and social development. *Developmental Review* 5:99–121, 1985.
   M. Rutter. Continuities and discontinuities from infancy, pp. 1256–1296. In J. Osofsky (editor), *Handbook of Infant Development.* New York: John Wiley & Sons, 1987.
   Werner and Smith, 1982 (note 9, above).
11. M. Rutter. Psychosocial resilience and protective mechanisms, pp. 181–214. *In* J. Rolf, A. S. Masten, D. Cicchetti, K. H. Nuechterlein, and S. Weintraub (editors), *Risk and Protective Factors in the Development of Psychopathology.* New York: Cambridge University Press, 1990.
12. L. A. Sroufe. The coherence of individual development. *American Psychologist* 34:834–841, 1979.
13. M. Bornstein and M. Sigman. Continuity in mental development from infancy. *Child Development*, 57: 251–274, 1986.
   J. Belsky, R. Lerner, and G. Spanier. *The Child in the Family.* Menlo Park, CA: Addison-Wesley, 1986.
14. Rutter, 1979 (note 9, above).
15. E. E. Werner. Vulnerability and resiliency in children at risk for delinquency: A longitudinal study from birth to adulthood, pp. 16–43. *In* J. D. Burchard and S. N. Burchard (editors), *Primary Prevention of Psychopathology: Vol. 10. Prevention of Delinquent Behavior.* Newbury Park, CA: Sage, 1987.
16. Werner and Smith, 1982 (note 9, above).
17. R. Marshall. *The State of Families, 3: Losing Direction, Families, Human Resource Development, and Economic Performance.* Milwaukee, WI: Family Service America, 1991.
18. E. Galinsky, J. T. Bond, and D. E. Friedman. *The Changing American Workforce: Highlights of the National Study.* New York: Families and Work Institute, 1993.

19. V. Fuchs. *Women's Quest for Economic Equality*. Cambridge, MA: Harvard University Press, 1988.

20. J. P. Robinson. *How Americans Use Time: A Social-Psychological Analysis of Everyday Behavior*. New York: Praeger, 1977.

    J.P. Robinson. Caring for kids. *American Demographics* 11(7):52, 1989.

21. A. Hochschild. *The Second Shift: Working Parents and the Revolution at Home*. New York: Viking, 1989.

22. S. Miller. *Early Childhood Services: A National Challenge*. New York: Ford Foundation, 1989.

23. M. Whitebook, D. Phillips, and C. Howes. *Who Cares? Child Care Teachers and the Quality of Care in America: National Child Care Staffing Study*. Oakland, CA: Child Care Employee Project, 1989.

    E. Galinsky, C. Howes, S. Kontos, and M. Shinn. The Study of Children in Family Child Care and Relative Care: Highlights of Findings. In process, to be published in 1994. New York: Families and Work Institute.

24. U.S. Bureau of the Census. *Child Support and Alimony: 1989*. Current Population Reports, Series P-60, No. 173. Washington, DC: U.S. Government Printing Office, 1991.

    W. Galston. Causes of declining well-being among U.S. children. *Aspen Institute Quarterly*, Winter 1993.

25. U.S. Bureau of the Census, 1991.

26. D. A. Dawson. Family Structure and Children's Health: United States, 1988. Vital and Health Statistics, Series 10, No. 178 (DHHS Pub. No. [PHS] 91-1506). Washington, DC: National Center for Health Statistics, 1991.

    C. D. Prince, C. W. Nord, and N. Zill. Social indicators predictive of school success: Linking health and social information available at birth to measures of children's health, behavior, and academic status. Paper presented at the annual meeting of the American Educational Research Association. Atlanta, GA, April 12–16, 1993.

27. S. S. McLanahan. The Two Faces of Divorce: Women's and Children's Interests. IRP discussion paper 903–89. Madison: University of Wisconsin, Institute for Research on Poverty, December 1989.

    F. F. Furstenberg and A. J. Cherlin. *Divided Families: What Happens to Children When Parents Part*. Cambridge, MA: Harvard University Press, 1991.

28. I. V. Sawhill. Young children and families. In *Setting Domestic Priorities: What Can Government Do?* Washington, DC: The Brookings Institution, 1992.

29. Ibid.

30. L. B. Williams and W. F. Pratt. Wanted and Unwanted Childbearing in the United States: 1973–88. Data from the National Survey of Family Growth. Advance Data from Vital and Health Statistics no. 189. Hyattsville, MD: National Center for Health Statistics, 1990.

31. D. L. Olds, C. R. Henderson, R. Tatelbaum, and R. Chamberlain. Improving the life-course development of socially disadvantaged mothers: A randomized trial of nurse home visitation. *American Journal of Public Health* 78:1436–1445, 1988.

32. S. L. Hofferth. Social and economic consequences of teenage childbearing, pp. 123–144. *In* Sandra L. Hofferth and Cheryl D. Hayes (editors), *Risking the Future: Adolescent Sexuality, Pregnancy, and Childbearing, vol. 2*. Washington, DC: National Academy Press, 1987.

33. M. Larner. Changes in network resources and relationships over time, pp. 181–204. *In* M. Cochran, M. Larner, D. Riley, L. Gunnarsson, and C. R. Henderson, Jr. (editors), *Extending Families: The Social Networks of Parents and Their Children*. Cambridge: Cambridge University Press, 1990.

34. Ibid.

35. F. Earls. Panel on Prevention of Violence and Violent Injuries. Position paper solicited by the Division of Injury Control, Centers for Disease Control. Atlanta, GA, April 1991.

36. N. Dubrow and J. Garbarino. Living in the war zone: Mothers and children in a public housing project. *Child Welfare* 68:3–20, 1988.

37. J. Osofsky. Violence in the lives of young children. Position paper prepared for the Carnegie Corporation Task Force on Meeting the Needs of Young Children. New York: Carnegie Corporation of New York, June 15, 1993.

38. L. Taylor, B. Zuckerman, V. Harik, and B. Groves. Witnessing violence by children and their mothers. *Journal of Developmental and Behavioral Pediatrics* (in press).

39. National Association for the Education of Young Children. NAEYC position statement on violence in the lives of children. *Young Children*, 48(6):80–84, September 1993.

40. S. D. Einbinder. A statistical profile of children living in poverty: Children under three and children under six, 1990. Unpublished document from the National Center for Children in Poverty. New York: Columbia University, School of Public Health, 1992.

41. Galston, 1993 (note 24, above).
42. S. K. Danziger and S. Danziger. Child poverty and public policy: Toward a comprehensive antipoverty agenda. *Daedalus* 122(1):57–84, Winter 1993.
43. National Commission on Children. *Speaking of Kids: A National Survey of Children and Parents.* Washington, DC, 1991.
44. General Accounting Office. Children and Youth. About 68,000 Homeless and 186,000 in Shared Housing at Any Given Time (GAO\PEMD-89-14). Washington, DC, 1989.
45. J. Garbarino. The meaning of poverty in the world of children. *American Behavioral Scientist* 35(3): 220–237, 1992.
46. Marshall, 1991 (note 17, above).
47. Ibid.
48. National Education Goals Panel, 1993 (note 1, above).
49. Marshall, 1991 (note 17, above).

PART II: STARTING POINTS FOR OUR YOUNGEST CHILDREN

Promote Responsible Parenthood

1. F. Earls and M. Carlson. Towards sustainable development for American families. *Daedalus* 122(1):93–121, 1993.
2. D. A. Hamburg. *Today's Children.* New York: Times Books, 1992.
3. L. B. Williams and W. F. Pratt. Wanted and unwanted childbearing in the United States: 1973–88. Data from the National Survey of Family Growth. *Advance Data from Vital and Health Statistics.* No. 189. Hyattsville, MD: National Center for Health Statistics, 1990.
4. Public Health Service Expert Panel on the Content of Prenatal Care. *Caring for Our Future: The Content of Prenatal Care.* Washington DC: U.S. Public Health Service, 1989, p. 25.
5. S. J. Zuravin. Unplanned pregnancies, family planning problems and child maltreatment. *Family Relations* 36:136–139, 1987.
Institute of Medicine. *Preventing Low Birth Weight.* Washington, DC: National Academy Press, 1985.
U.S. Public Health Service. *Healthy People 2000: National Health Promotion and Disease Prevention Objectives.* DHHS Publication Number (PHS) 91–50212. Washington, DC: U.S. Department of Health and Human Services, 1990, p. 191.
6. Alan Guttmacher Institute. Facts in Brief: Teenage Sexual and Reproductive Behavior. New York, July 15, 1993.
7. I. V. Sawhill. Young children and families. *In Setting Domestic Priorities: What Can Government Do?* Washington, DC: The Brookings Institution, July 1992.
8. G. C. Adams and R. C. Williams. *Sources of Support for Adolescent Mothers.* Washington, DC: Congressional Budget Office, September 1990.
9. S. L. Hofferth. Social and economic consequences of teenage childbearing, pp.123–144. In S. L. Hofferth and C. D. Hayes (editors), *Risking the Future: Adolescent Sexuality, Pregnancy, and Childbearing,* vol. 2. Washington, DC: National Academy Press, 1987.
10. Sawhill, 1992 (note 7, above).
11. Alan Guttmacher Institute. Washington memo: Prevention strategies discussed for teens at risk—House hearing on adolescent pregnancy focuses on social and economic costs. Washington, DC, December 1992.
12. Alan Guttmacher Institute, 1993 (note 6, above).
13. Institute of Medicine, 1985 (note 5 above).
14. B. Jack and L. Culpepper. Preconception care. *In* I. R. Merkatz, and J. E. Thompson (editors), *New Perspectives on Prenatal Care.* New York: Elsevier, 1990.
15. R. B. Gold and D. Daley. Public funding of contraceptive, sterilization and abortion services, fiscal year 1990. *Family Planning Perspectives* 23:204–211, 1991.
16. Ibid.
17. J. A. Davis and T. W. Smith. *General Social Surveys, 1972–1993.* Chicago: National Opinion Research Center, 1993.
Twenty-second Annual Gallup Poll of the Public's Attitudes towards Public Schools. *Phi Delta Kappa* 72(1):42–55, September 1990.
18. Public Health Service Expert Panel on the Content of Prenatal Care, 1989 (note 4, above).
19. U.S. Public Health Service, 1990 (note 5 above).
20. Jack and Culpepper, 1990 (note 14, above).
21. A. Kempe *et al.* Clinical determinants of the racial disparity in very low birthweight. *New England Journal of Medicine* 327(14):969–973, 1992.
22. P. D. Mullen and M. A. Glenday. Alcohol avoidance counselling in prenatal care. *In* I. R. Merkatz and J. E. Thompson (editors), *New Perspectives on Prenatal Care.* New York: Elsevier, 1990.
23. J. Rosenblith. *In the Beginning: Development from Conception to Age Two.* Newbury Park: Sage Publications, 1992.
24. E. Pollitt and K. Gorman. Nutritional deficiencies as developmental risk factors. Paper presented at the Twenty-seventh Minnesota Symposium on Child Psychology, "Infants and Children at Risk." Minneapolis: Institute of Child Development, University of Minnesota, October 1992.

25. U.S. Public Health Service, 1990 (note 5, above).

26. T. V. Ellerbrock, T. J. Bush, M. E. Chamberland, and M. J. Oxtoby. Epidemiology of Women with AIDS in the United States, 1981 through 1990. *Journal of the American Medical Association* 265:2971–2975, 1991.

27. B. Zuckerman, H. Amaro, H. Bauchner, and H. Cabral. Depressive symptoms during pregnancy: Relationship to poor health behaviors. *American Journal of Obstetrics and Gynecology* 160:1107–1111, 1989.

28. D. J. Willis and E. W. Holden. *Developmental Assessment in Clinical Child Psychology: A Handbook.* New York: Pergamon Press, 1990.

29. Institute of Medicine, 1985 (note 5, above).
M.C. McCormick, J. Brooks-Gunn, K. Workman-Daniels, J. Turner, G.J. Peckham. The health and developmental status of very low-birth-weight children at school age. *Journal of the American Medical Association.* 267(16):2204–2207.

30. N. Garmezy and M. Rutter (editors). *Stress, Coping and Development in Children.* Baltimore: John Hopkins University Press, 1988.

31. Institute of Medicine, 1985 (note 5, above).

32. National Center for Health Statistics. Health Aspects of Pregnancy and Childbirth, United States 1982. DHHS Publ. No. (PHS) 99–1992. Hyattsville, MD: U.S. Public Health Service, 1988.
Institute of Medicine. *Prenatal Care: Reaching Mothers, Reaching Infants.* Washington, DC: National Academy Press, 1988.
National Center for Health Statistics. *Health, United States, 1992.* Hyattsville, MD: U.S. Public Health Service, 1993.

33. U.S. Congress, Office of Technology Assessment. *Healthy Children: Investing in the Future.* OTA-H-345. Washington, DC: U.S. Government Printing Office, February 1988.

34. S. M. Dornbusch, J. A. Barr, and N. A. Seer. The impact of education for parenting upon parents, children and family systems. A report prepared for the Task Force on Meeting the Needs of Young Children. New York: Carnegie Corporation of New York, February 1993.

35. Ibid.

36. Hamburg, 1992 (note 2, above).

37. D. L. Olds, C. R. Henderson, C. Phelps, H. Kitzman, and C. Hanks. Effect of prenatal care and infancy nurse home visitation on government spending. *Medical Care* 31:155–174, 1993.

38. R. Halpern. Parent support and education programs. *Children and Youth Services Review* 12:285–308, 1990.
R. Halpern. Community-based early intervention. In S. Meisels and J. Shonkoff (editors), *Handbook of Early Childhood Intervention.* New York: Cambridge University Press, 1990.

Guarantee Quality Child Care Choices

1. S. L. Hofferth, A. Brayfield, S. Deich, and P. Holcomb. *The National Child Care Survey 1990.* Washington, DC: The Urban Institute, 1991.

2. P. Hopper and E. Zigler. The medical and social science basis for a national infant care leave policy. *American Journal of Orthopsychiatry* 38(3):324–336, 1988.

3. E. F. Zigler and M. Frank (editors). *The Parental Leave Crisis: Toward a National Policy.* New Haven: Yale University Press, 1988.

4. Ibid.

5. J. T. Bond and E. Galinsky. Parental leave benefits for American workers: Strengthening federal parental leave policy. Paper prepared for the Task Force on Meeting the Needs of Young Children. New York: Carnegie Corporation of New York, January 1993.
J. T. Bond, E. Galinsky, M. Lord, G. L. Staines, and K. R. Brown. *Beyond the Parental Leave Debate: The Impact of Laws in Four States.* New York: Families and Work Institute, 1991.

6. Ibid.

7. E. Galinsky, D. Friedman, and C. Hernandez. *The Corporate Reference Guide to Work–Family Programs.* New York: Families and Work Institute, 1991.
E. Galinsky, J. T. Bond, and D. E. Friedman. *The Changing American Workforce: Highlights of the National Study.* New York: Families and Work Institute, 1993.

8. E. Galinsky and A. Morris. Employers and child care. *Pediatrics* 91(1, Supplement Issue):209–217, 1993.
E. Galinsky. Families and work. *In* S. L. Kagan and B. Weissbourd (editors), *Putting Families First: America's Family Support Movement and the Challenge of Change.* San Francisco: Jossey-Bass, Inc., in press.

9. Hofferth et al., 1991 (note 1 above).
Child Care Action Campaign. Choosing quality child care: A qualitative study conducted in Houston, Hartford, West Palm Beach, Charlotte, Alameda, Los Angeles, Salem and Minneapolis. New York, January 1992.

10. M. Whitebook, C. Howes, and D. Phillips. *Who Cares? Child Care Teachers and the Quality of Care in America*. Final Report of the National Child Care Staffing Study. Oakland, CA: Child Care Employee Project, 1989.

    E. Galinsky, C. Howes, S. Kontos, and M. Shinn. *The Study of Children in Family Child Care and Relative Care: Highlights of Findings*. In process, to be published in 1994. New York: Families and Work Institute.

11. K. T. Young, E. Marx, and E. Zigler. Is quality reflected in infant and toddler child care regulations? Paper presented at the biennial meeting of the Society for Research in Child Development. Seattle, April 1991.

12. Ibid.

13. Whitebook *et al.*, 1989 (note 10, above).

    Galinsky *et al.*, 1994 (note 10, above).

14. G. Morgan, S. Azer, J. B. Costley, A. Genser, I. F. Goodman, J. Lombardi, and B. McGimsey. *Making A Career of It: The State of the States Report on Career Development in Early Care and Education*. Boston, MA: The Center for Career Development in Early Care and Education at Wheelock College, 1993.

15. M. Whitebook, D. Phillips, and C. Howes. *National Child Care Staffing Study Revisited: Four Years in the Life of Center-Based Child Care*. San Francisco: Child Care Employee Project, 1993.

16. B. Willer, S. L. Hofferth, E. E. Kisker, P. Divine-Hawkins, E. Farquar, and F. B. Glantz (editors). *The Demand and Supply of Child Care in 1990: Joint Findings from the National Child Care Survey 1990 and a Profile of Child Care Settings*. Washington, DC: National Association for the Education of Young Children, 1991.

17. B. Willer. Estimating the full cost of quality, pp. 55–86. In B. Willer (editor), *Reaching the Full Cost of Quality*. Washington, DC: National Association for the Education of Young Children, 1990.

18. J. Garbarino. The meaning of poverty in the world of children. *American Behavioral Scientist* 35(3): 220–237, 1992.

19. Committee for Economic Development. *Why Child Care Matters: Preparing Young Children for a More Productive America*. New York: Committee for Economic Development, 1993.

20. Hofferth *et al.*, 1991 (note 1, above).

21. Willer *et al.*, 1991 (note 16, above).

22. M. L. Culkin, S. W. Helburn, and J. R. Morris. Current price versus full cost: An economic perspective pp. 9–26. *In* Willer, 1990 (note 17, above).

23. Willer *et al.*, 1991 (note 16, above).

24. Child Care Action Campaign, 1992 (note 9, above).

25. S. Hofferth. Child care in the 1990's. Paper prepared for the meeting of the Congressional Commission on Immigration Reform. Washington, DC, February 26, 1993.

26. Hofferth *et al.*, 1991 (note 1, above).

27. Child Care Action Campaign, 1992 (note 9, above).

28. R. O. Barnes. The distributional effects of alternative child care programs. Paper prepared for the tenth annual meeting of the Association for Public Policy Analysis and Management, Seattle, Washington, October 27–29, 1988. Washington, DC: The Urban Institute, 1988.

29. Committee for Economic Development, 1993 (note 20, above).

30. E. Galinsky, D. Friedman, and J. Lombardi. A quality early childhood system for the 21st century: A working paper. New York: Families and Work Institute, December 1992.

31. C. D. Hayes, J. L. Palmer, and M. J. Zaslow (editors). *Who Cares for America's Children? Child Care Policy for the 1990's*. Washington DC: National Academy Press, 1990, pp. 95–96.

Ensure Good Health and Protection

1. Office of Disease Prevention, U.S. Public Health Service. *Disease Prevention/Health Promotion: The Facts*. Palo Alto, CA: Bull Publishing Company, 1988.

2. A. Evans and R. B. Friedland. Financing and delivery of health care for children. Paper prepared for the Advisory Panel on Health Care Financing: Policy and Administrative Choices. Washington, DC: National Academy of Social Insurance, 1993.

3. U.S. Congress, Office of Technology Assessment. *Healthy Children: Investing in the Future*. OTA-H-345. Washington, DC: U.S. Government Printing Office, 1988. pp. 11–14.

4. U.S. Congress, Office of Technology Assessment, 1988 (note 3, above).

5. U.S. Department of Health and Human Services, Centers for Disease Control. Advance report of measles surveillance statistics. *Morbidity and Mortality Weekly Report* 42(42)813–815, October 1993.

6. Ibid.

7. R. Sampson. Family management and child development: Insights from social disorganization theory, pp. 63–93. *In* Jean McCord (editor), *Advances in Criminological Theory*, Volume 3. New Brunswick, NJ: Transaction, 1993.

8. D. Frank, M. Napoleone, A. Meyers, N. Roos, and K. Peterson. A heat or eat effect? Seasonal changes in weight for age in a pediatric emergency room. Paper delivered at the Annual Meeting of the American Public Health Association. Atlanta, GA, 1991.

9. J. Y. Jones. *Child Nutrition Issues: 1990–91*. Congressional Research Service Issue Brief, order code IB90115. Washington, DC: U.S. Congress, Library of Congress, September 27, 1990. p. 5.

10. A. Meyers, D. Rubin, M. Napoleone, and K. Nichols. Public housing subsidies may improve poor children's nutrition. Letter to the editor. *American Journal of Public Health* 83(1):115, January 1993.

11. H. Needleman, A. Schell, D. Bellinger, A. Leviton, and E. Allred. The long-term effects of exposure to low doses of lead in childhood. *New England Journal of Medicine* 322(2):83–88, 1990.

12. M. Moon. Overview: Setting the context for reform. *The Future of Children: Health Care Reform* 3(2):23–36, Summer/Fall 1993.

13. Families USA Foundation. Half of Us: Families Priced Out of Health Protection. Washington, DC, 1993.

14. U.S. Congress, Congressional Research Service. *Health Insurance and The Uninsured: Background Data and Analysis*. Congressional Research Service Report for Congress, Education and Labor ser. no. 100-z. Washington, DC, 1988, p. 66.

15. American Academy of Pediatrics, National Commission to Prevent Infant Mortality, National Commission on Children, and House Select Committee on Children, Youth and Families. Child health in 1990: The United States compared to Canada, England and Wales, France, the Netherlands, and Norway. *Pediatrics* 86 (Supplement 6):1025–1127, 1990.

16. Ibid.

17. Congressional Budget Office. Statement of Nancy Gordon before the Subcommittee on Health, House Committee on Ways and Means, U.S. Congress, January 26, 1993. Cited in Moon, 1993 (note 12, above).

18. E. J. Jameson and E. Wehr. Drafting national health care reform legislation to protect the health interests of children. *Stanford Law and Policy Review* 5(1):152–176, 1993.

19. The Select Panel for the Promotion of Child Health. *Better Health for Our Children: A National Strategy. Volume I: Major Findings and Recommendations*. Washington, DC: Public Health Service, U.S. Department of Health and Human Services, 1981.

20. Jameson and Wehr, 1993 (note 18, above).

21. S. S. Brown. Health care benefits for children: Their content and cost. Working policy paper prepared for the Carnegie Task Force on Meeting the Needs of Young Children. New York: Carnegie Corporation of New York, 1993.

22. U.S. General Accounting Office. Home visiting: A promising early intervention strategy for at-risk families. Report to the Chairman, Subcommittee on Labor, Health and Human Services, Education, and Related Agencies, Committee on Appropriations, U.S. Senate. GAO/HRD-90-83. Washington, DC: U.S. Government Printing Office, July 1990.

23. D. L. Olds, C. R. Henderson, C. Phelps, H. Kitzman, and C. Hanks. Effect of prenatal and infancy nurse home visitation on government spending. *Medical Care* 31:155–174, 1993.
   H. C. Heins, N. W. Nance, and J. E. Furguson. Social support in improving perinatal outcome: The Resource Mothers program. *Obstetrics and Gynecology* 70:(2)263–266, 1987.

24. Ibid.

25. Evans and Friedland, 1993 (note 2, above).
   National Center for Health Statistics. *Health United States and Prevention Profile, 1991*. Hyattsville, MD, 1992.

26. M. H. Wilson, S. P. Baker, S. P. Teret, S. Shock, and J. Garbarino. *Saving Children: A Guide to Injury Prevention*. New York: Oxford University Press, 1991.

27. Metropolitan Life Insurance Company. Major causes of accident mortality among children: United States, 1988. *Statistical Bulletin* 73(1):2–9, 1992.

28. Wilson et al., 1991 (note 28, above).

29. N. A. Vanderpool. Young children and families: Creating a social policy agenda; a review of selected reports. Paper prepared for the Task Force on Meeting the Needs of Young Children. New York: Carnegie Corporation of New York, 1993.

30. D. A. Hamburg. *Today's Children*. New York: Times Books, 1992.

31. National Commission on Children. *Beyond Rhetoric: A New American Agenda for Children and Families*. Washington, DC, 1991. p. 132, Chapter 6.

32. Hamburg, 1992 (note 30, above).

33. M. A. Fenley, J. Gaiter, L. C. Hammett, L. C. Liburd, J. A. Mercy, P. W. O'Carroll, C. Onwuachi-Saunders, K. E. Powell, and T. Thornton. *The Prevention of Youth Violence: A Framework for Community Action*. Atlanta: Centers for Disease Control and Prevention, 1993.

34. D. Cicchetti and M. Lynch. Toward an ecological/transactional model of community violence and child maltreatment: Consequences for children's development. *Psychiatry: Interpersonal and Biological Processes* 56(1):96–118, February 1993.

35. R. Gelles. *Intimate Violence: The Definitive Study of the Causes and Consequences of Abuse in the American Family*. New York: Simon and Schuster, 1988.

36. L. Bulluck, and J. McFarlane. The prevalence and characteristics of battered women in a primary care setting. *Health Care Issues* 14:49–55, 1989.
A. Satin, D. Hemsell, I. Stone, S. Theriot, and G. Wendel. Sexual assault in pregnancy. *American Journal of Obstetrics and Gynecology* 77:710–714, 1991.

37. A. S. Helton, J. McFarlane, and E. T. Anderson. Battered and pregnant: A prevalence study. *American Journal of Public Health* 77(10):1337–1339, 1987.

38. U.S. Department of Health and Human Services. National Child Abuse and Neglect Data System: Working paper 1. Publication No. (ACF) 92-30361. 1992.

39. Ibid.

40. D. Daro and K. McCurdy. *Current Trends in Child Abuse Reporting and Fatalities: The Results of the 1990 Annual Fifty-State Survey*. Chicago: National Committee for the Prevention of Child Abuse, 1990.

41. B. A. Younger. Infants' detection of correlations among feature categories. *Child Development* 61:(3)614–620, 1990.

42. J. D. Osofsky and E. Fenichel (editors). *Caring for Infants in Violent Environments: Hurt, Healing, and Hope*. Arlington, VA: Zero to Three/National Center for Clinical Infant Programs, 1994.

43. J. P. Kassirer. Guns in the household. *New England Journal of Medicine* 329:1117–1118, 1993.

Mobilize Communities to Support Young Children and Their Families

1. K. T. Young and E. Marx. What Does Learning Mean for Infants and Toddlers? The Contributions of the Child, the Family, and the Community. Report no. 3, Center for Families, Communities, and Schools and Children's Learning, Washington, DC: U.S. Department of Education, 1992.

2. U. Bronfenbrenner. *The Ecology of Human Development: Experiments by Nature and Design*. Cambridge, MA: Harvard University Press, 1979.

3. M. Cochran, M. Larner, D. Riley, L. Gunnarsson, and C. R. Henderson, Jr. *Extending Families: The Social Networks of Parents and their Children*. New York: Cambridge University Press, 1990.

4. R. Sampson. Family management and child development: Insights from social disorganization theory, pp. 63–93. *In* Jean McCord (editor), *Advances in Criminological Theory*, Volume 3. New Brunswick, NJ: Transaction, 1993.

5. National Association of State Boards of Education. *Caring Communities: Supporting Young Children and Families, Report of the National Task Force on School Readiness*. Alexandria, VA, 1991.

6. E. Galinsky, D. Friedman, and J. Lombardi. A Quality Early Childhood System for the 21st Century. A working paper. New York: Families and Work Institute, December 1992.

7. I. Sawhill. Young children and families, pp. 147–184. In *Setting Domestic Priorities: What Can Government Do?* Washington, DC: The Brookings Institution, 1992.

8. M. L. Allen, P. Brown, and B. Finlay. *Helping Children by Strengthening Families: A Look at Family Support Programs*. Washington, DC: Children's Defense Fund, 1992.
L. Schorr and D. Schorr. *Within Our Reach: Breaking the Cycle of Disadvantage*. New York: Doubleday, 1988.
H. B. Weiss and F. H. Jacobs (editors). *Evaluating Family Programs*. New York: Aldine de Gruyter, 1988.

9. E. Zigler and S. Muenchow. *Head Start: The Inside Story of America's Most Successful Educational Experiment*. New York: Basic Books, 1992.

10. Galinsky *et al.*, 1992 (note 6, above).

11. National Performance Review. *From Red Tape to Results: Creating a Government That Works Better and Costs Less*. Washington, DC: U.S. Government Printing Office, 1993.

Austin (Texas) Project, 89

Avance program (Texas), 38, 95

Banks, child care programs and, 57

Better Babies, 95

Birth to Three program (Oregon), 38

Boston City Hospital, Child Witness to Violence Program, 77

    Reach Out and Read (ROAR) program, 75

California Child Care Initiative, 53

"Caring for Tomorrow's Children" (South Carolina), 34

Center for Successful Child Development (Chicago), 91

Chicago, Erikson Institute violence seminars, 77

"Child Care Aware," Dayton Hudson Corp., 57

Child care career development program, 53

Child Care Initiative, California, 53

    United Way of Massachusetts Bay, 57

Child Development and Community Policing (New Haven, Conn.), 77

Child and Family Neighborhood Program (Syracuse, N.Y.), 87–88

Child Witness to Violence Program (Boston City Hospital), 77

Children's Initiative, the (Pew Charitable Trusts), 91

Colorado, "First Impressions" initiative, 100

    Strategic Plan for Families and Children, 100

Communities for Child Safety (National 4-H Council), 73, 74

Crèches familiales, in France, 60

Dayton Hudson Corp., "Child Care Aware," 57

    "Family-to-Family," 57

Delaware, child care career development program, 53

District of Columbia, Maternity Outreach Mobile Van, 34

Early Childhood Family Education program (Minnesota), 40

Educational Home Model Outreach Program (Montana), 53

Edward C. Mazique Parent–Child Center (Washington, D.C.), 96

Elmira, N.Y., Prenatal and Infancy Home Visiting Program, 35

Evanston, Ill., Family Focus Program, 36

Every Child By Two Campaign, 67

Erikson Institute violence seminars, 77

"Family-to-Family," Dayton Hudson Corp., 57

Family Focus Program (Evanston, Ill.), 36

Family Preservation and Support Services Program, 41

Family Resource Centers (Kentucky), 40

"First Impressions" (Colorado), 100

France, crèches familiales, 60

Friends of the Family (Maryland), 40

Georgia, Nurse Midwifery Project, 34

Governor's Cabinet on Children and Families (West Virginia), 100

Head Start, 95–99

Health Care Access Act (Louisiana), 34

Healthy Families America, 72

Healthy Start Program (Hawaii) 65, 72, 95

Human Biology Middle Grades Life Sciences Project, 30

Illinois Facilities Fund, 57

Immunization project, San Antonio, 65

Kentucky Education Reform Act of 1990, 40

Kiwanis Club programs, 91

Louisiana Health Care Access Act, 34

Maryland, Friends of the Family, 40

Maternity Outreach Mobile Van (District of Columbia), 34

Minnesota, Early Childhood Family Education program, 40

Missouri, Parents As Teachers program, 40, 41

Montana, Educational Home Model Outreach Program, 53

National 4-H Council, Communities for Child
    Safety, 73, 74
New Haven, Conn., police violence program, 77
    Polly T. McCabe Center, 35
North Carolina, T.E.A.C.H. project, 55
Nurse Midwifery Project (Georgia), 34

Oregon, Birth to Three program, 38
Ounce of Prevention Fund, 91

Parents As Teachers program (Missouri), 40, 41, 94, 95
Parent–Child Centers, 94, 95, 96
Pew Charitable Trusts, the Children's Initiative, 91
Polly T. McCabe Center (New Haven, Conn.), 35
Prenatal and Infancy Home Visiting Program
    (Elmira, N.Y.), 35

Reach Out and Read (ROAR), at Boston City
    Hospital, 75
Resource Mothers programs (South Carolina), 41

San Antonio, immunization project, 65
Schools of the 21st Century, 94
Smart Start, 95
South Carolina, "Caring for Tommorrow's
    Children," 34
    Resource Mothers program, 41
Southern Regional Project on Infant Mortality, 34
Special Supplemental Food Program for Women,
    Infants and Children (WIC), 66
Stanford University Human Biology Middle Grades Life
    Science Project, 30
Success by Six, 95
Syracuse, N.Y., Child and Family Neighborhood
    Program, 87–88

T.E.A.C.H. project (North Carolina), 55
Texas, Avance program, 38

U.S. Army child care system, 55
United Way of Massachusetts Bay, Child Care
    Initiative, 57

WIC program, 66
Washington, D.C., Edward C. Mazique Parent–Child
    Center, 96
West Virginia, Governor's Cabinet on Children and
    Families, 100

Yale Child Study Center, New Haven police
    program, 77